Wandering in American Deserts
Discovery, Visions, Redemption

Other Wanderland Writers Anthologies

2010 *Wandering in Costa Rica: Landscapes Lost and Found*

2012 *Wandering in Bali: A Tropical Paradise Discovered*

2013 *Wandering in Paris: Luminaries and Love in the City of Light* (First Place, London Book Festival Awards; Honorable Mention, Paris Book Festival Awards)

2015 *Wandering in Cornwall: Mystery, Mirth and Transformation in the Land of Ancient Celts* (IndieFab Winner, Foreword's Book of the Year Awards; Finalist, Next Generation Indie Book Awards; Honorable Mention, London Book Festival Awards; Honorable Mention, Paris Book Festival Awards)

2016 *Wandering in Andalusia: The Soul of Southern Spain* (Second Place, San Francisco Book Festival Awards)

2018 *Wandering in Cuba: Revolution and Beyond*

2020 *Wandering in Greece: Athens, Islands and Antiquities* (Next Generation Indie Finalist)

2022 *Wandering in Japan: The Spirit of Tokyo, Kyoto and Beyond* (Silver award, National Association of Travel Journalists; Distinguished Favorite, Independent Press Award; Finalist, Next Generation Indie Book Awards; Honorable Mention, Paris Book Festival; Runner Up, San Francisco Book Festival)

WANDERING IN AMERICAN DESERTS
Discovery, Visions, Redemption

Edited by
Linda Watanabe McFerrin,
Joanna Biggar and
Laurie McAndish King

Wanderland Writers
Oakland, California

Copyright © 2024 Wanderland Writers. All rights reserved.
No part of this publication may be reproduced, distributed, or transmitted in any form or by any means, including photocopying, recording, or other electronic or mechanical methods, without the prior written permission of the publisher, except in the case of brief quotations embodied in critical reviews and certain other noncommercial uses permitted by copyright law.

For permission to print essays in this volume, grateful acknowledgement is made to the holders of copyright named on pages 192-203.

The poems "Hands" and "Lost Horse Valley" were previously published in *Invisible Gifts* by Manic D Press (2018).

Photographs are in public domain, except as noted:
Front cover and pages xx, 80, 86, 104, 110 © Laurie McAndish King
Pages 10, 38 © Cyndi Goddard
Page 28 © Anne Sigmon
Page 64 Photo of Preckwinkle—from a poster at the Agua Caliente Cultural Museum in Palm Springs, California
Page 128 © Linda Watanabe McFerrin
Page 148 © Tatum Tomlinson
Page 162 © Naomi Lopez
Back cover © Doug Hale

Wikimedia Commons: The pottery used as an icon is an image of an Anasazi olla (jar) made between 1100 and 1250 in the Four Corners region of the American southwest; page 18: inkknife_2000; page 20: Renee Grayson; page 26: Nikhil More; page 46: Ltshears; page 54: Carol M. Highsmith; page 74: Edward S. Curtis; page 96: Dietmar Rabich; page 120: Pierre André Leclercq; page 134: real Kam75 (moon) and Retron (wolf); page 140: Bernard Spragg; page 154: Dllu; page 170: Panzerhorgen; page 178: National Park Service; page 186: PiConsti.

Cover design, interior design and map by Jim Shubin.

CATALOGING DATA:
Wandering in American Deserts: Discovery, Visions, Redemption
Edited by Linda Watanabe McFerrin, Joanna Biggar and Laurie McAndish King

ISBN: 979-8-9887021-6-0
First printing 2024
Printed in the United States of America

Contents

Introduction	x
Foreword by Tim Cahill	xiv

DISCOVERY

Chasing Mirage in the Imperial Valley Hugh Biggar	1
Desert Pas de Deux Cyndi Goddard	11
Lost Horse Valley Maw Shein Win	19
A Party on Camelback Mountain Tom Harrell	21
Hands Maw Shein Win	27
Orders of Magnitude Anne Sigmon	29
Valley of the Future Cyndi Goddard	39
She-Lizards of the Chiricahua Desert Laurie McAndish King	47
Christmas in Death Valley Linda Watanabe McFerrin	55
Finding Cahuilla Madeleine Adkins	65
The Girl Who Swallowed Words Joanna Biggar	75

VISIONS

Salvation Mountain, A Love Story Joanna Biggar		81
The Wizard of East Jesus Laurie McAndish King		87
Nankoweap for Me Judy Zimola		97
Old Boots, New Vision Peg Wendling Gerdes		105
Blissed Out at the Integratron Laurie McAndish King		111
The Shaman's Cave MJ Pramik		121
Brommer's Palette Linda Watanabe McFerrin		129

REDEMPTION

Peak Experiences on a Desert Plain Daphne Beyers — 135

From Sedona to Flagstaff and Back:
The Road to Redemption Joanna Biggar — 141

Step by Step at the Grand Staircase-Escalante
Tatum Tomlinson — 149

Borrego Springs' Field of Dreams Michael J. Fitzgerald — 155

White Sands and Silence Naomi Lopez — 163

Poetic Justice Judy Zimola — 171

Chaco Canyon: A Desert Redemption J. R. Barnett — 179

Night Sky Linda Watanabe McFerrin — 187

Author Biographies — 192
Editor Biographies — 201

North American Deserts

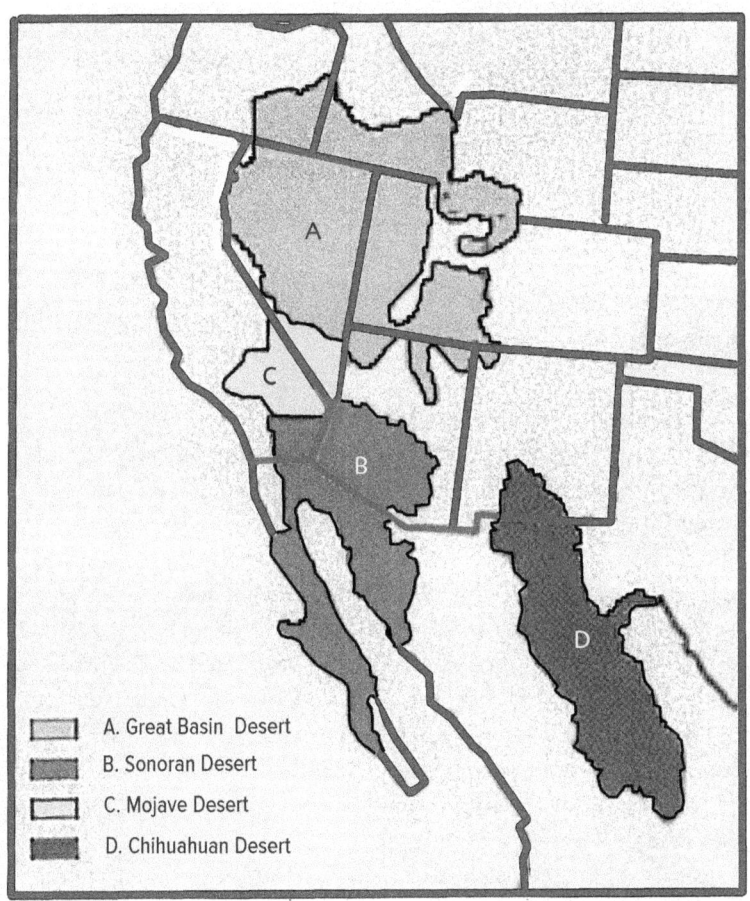

- A. Great Basin Desert
- B. Sonoran Desert
- C. Mojave Desert
- D. Chihuahuan Desert

The largest of North America's four great deserts is the **Great Basin**, a high, "cold" desert in a dry basin that's completely isolated from the world's oceans. It includes the Colorado Plateau Desert. The **Mojave**, a desert in the rain shadow of the southern Sierra Nevada mountains, encompasses the hottest place in North America: Death Valley. The **Sonoran Desert** averages ten intense *haboobs*, or giant dust storms, per summer, during which sand and dust can reach up to 10,000 feet. The high-altitude **Chihuahuan Desert** is one of the most diverse arid regions in the world.

Introduction

Whether or not we have ever visited a desert, we all carry within us our imagined Saharas—dry, harsh and barren, wastelands of unremitting emptiness. But once we set foot in one, we find something else—vast spaces filled with life, beauty and serenity; perhaps mysticism, in the way of all spiritual seekers; perhaps sacred connections to ancestors, in the way of Native Americans. In America, western deserts comprise so much of our country—Texas, Oklahoma, New Mexico, Arizona, Colorado, Utah, Nevada, California—that once we go there, we encounter no wasteland, but a staggering variety of landscapes, animal life, plants, and geographical and human history that leave trails for us to follow into the present.

In this volume, we sample widely. We visit strange flora, such as the Joshua tree, which the Mormons named after the armies of the biblical Joshua marching in the desert. We see odd natural formations, such as rock caves fit for shamans; earth reshaped by the force of earthquakes; an ancient sea brought to life by human folly; the night sky as it was in the beginning. We encounter birds, coyotes and parthenogenetic she-lizards. We hear the power of silence.

Importantly, we meet other humans of every kind: members of the present-day Cahuilla tribe who share their music and culture, pop singers and cowboy poets, inventors and artists, and eccentrics who seem to thrive in the desert air: wizards, drop-outs, a misfit who finds salvation in painting a mountain.

The writers who bring their insights to this volume represent, like the desert itself, great diversity. They vary in age, places visited, and the time and purpose of their travels. One came to celebrate Christmas and plunged into a past of ghost towns and old saloons. Another came deliberately seeking the past while pursuing the trail of an ancient shaman; yet another sought it through the wisdom of the Cahuilla people. Still others visited the same place, the Salton Sea, and found very different things—the vision of a lost paradise, versus a vision of the future in harvesting lithium. Many came looking for answers and encountered strange delights: a fantastic machine, artists, eccentrics, a self-proclaimed wizard. And others came, as seekers often do, in search of themselves: a man in search of his father, a lonely college student wanting community, a lost teen seeking her soul.

But whatever quest brings us to the desert, we've all experienced its contradictions, its surprises, its ability to turn dry sand into glorious bloom. Beneath the vast canopy of desert sky, by day its creatures manage their lives under a dome of heat; by night they shiver in awe under a canopy of frigid stars. And even as we contemplate majestic rock canyons and burning sands stretching into the mirage of a horizon, we must remind ourselves that we are at the bottom of long-disappeared seas. Just as dried-up seabeds, bones and fossils offer up cautionary tales of cataclysmic changes in the past, with every step we take, we cannot avoid recognizing the cataclysmic changes of the present. With climate change and its unimaginably high temperatures, drought, its die-offs and the encroaching desertification of much of our habitable world, we can only strive to learn the lessons the desert has to teach us. And quickly, before we have no choice.

*—Linda Watanabe McFerrin, Joanna Biggar,
and Laurie McAndish King
Oakland, California and Novato, California*

Foreword

This, dear reader, is a book of top-notch stories about the American Desert. There are, in fact, several distinct deserts that span the country. The vast sea of sagebrush that covers large swaths of Nevada, Utah, and Oregon is called the Great Basin Desert. The Sonoran Desert of southern Arizona, with its abundant wildlife and flowering cacti, is almost lush as deserts go; the Colorado Plateau Desert is a wonderland of mesas and canyons such as seen in Road Runner cartoons. The Chihuahuan Desert in New Mexico and Texas is a fierce high-elevation desert a person wants to see on horseback in the company of genuine cowboys.

You will encounter these deserts and the people who live in them in the pages that follow.

The editors have asked me to introduce this book with a story of my own that takes place in the hottest of the American Deserts, the Mojave.

To wit:

On a blistering hot August night a few decades ago, I found myself trudging across the Badwater Basin, in Death Valley. This is the lowest point in North America and, arguably, the hottest place on

Foreword — Tim Cahill

earth. I had a desire, at the time, to experience various degrees of extremity, and Death Valley fit the bill. My planned route would take me from Badwater, at 282 feet below sea level, to the summit of Mount Whitney, which, at 14,505 feet, is the highest point in the lower 48. That summit was a little over 100 miles away and 14,787 above my present location.

I chose to make the trip during the hottest time of year because I lacked the technical skills needed to climb Whitney during its time of ice and snow. That meant traversing 100 miles of the hottest desert on earth at the hottest time of the year, which is why I decided to walk in the cool of the night.

The overland route ran west, through the vast and arid Panamint Valley, and led eventually into the Owens Valley at the foot of Whitney. The trek took about two weeks, and when I eventually set up camp on Whitney's broad summit, grand epiphanies, as usual, failed to epiphanize. I looked back over my route, recalled this or that hardship, and thought, "I like the desert. I like how it makes me feel and how it makes me think."

For instance, I love the way the desert quantifies the calculus of desire. During the dry sandblasted days, when the circling winds spin dust devils in the near distance, it is best to find shelter. An open-sided tarp, a lean-to, will work to block both the sun and the convection-oven blasts of wind. A canyon gouged into rock by some long-defunct stream is an ideal shelter. These canyons are sinuous in shape, so there is always a shadow as the desiccating sun moves overhead. If you have water, that's all you want and all you need. Water and shade. That's it.

As the sun sets, the land, which looked so harsh and unforgiving, softens as it takes on various pastels. Rocks sometimes glitter in slanting pillars of God-light. The western sky bleeds out a rainbow that colors both the denuded land and the sharp, angry mountains. It's beautiful. The temperature moderates and want enters the equation. An iced tea will come to mind. Or a cold beer. Something to eat other than camp food. Someone to share this with. Kindness. Peace on earth. Love. Is that too much to ask?

The next day's response is in the negative. The sun rises fierce and angry. The land, stripped of vegetation, reveals its various faults. There are impossible distances in all directions, and the sense of isolation is without bounds. Indigenous people, the Timbisha Shoshone, had many names for this place and one of them is "ground on fire." The winds are constant, parching, dehydrating. The need for water asserts itself.

And soon enough, there is no want other than need.

It occurred to me that this precarious balance of want and need is an invitation to introspection, a flat-out temptation to commit philosophy. I think this is why many religions—Judaism, Christianity, Islam—arose out of the desert. And it is the reason why, after I suffered a near-death experience rafting the Grand Canyon—after I spent five days in an Intensive Care Unit—I chose to go to Death Valley to recuperate. There were a few newspaper articles about my mishap and current location. The most asked question was "Who goes to Death Valley to recuperate?"

I do.

I have my reasons.

—Tim Cahill
Livingston, Montana

Discovery

A faded billboard advertising Bombay Beach

Chasing Mirage in the Imperial Valley

Hugh Biggar

At a dusty crossroads in Brawley, California, I came across my first indicator that life in the Imperial Valley desert is not always on the level.

On my way to a work meeting, I pulled over to check directions on Google Maps and saw that someone had pinned a spot notable for being both odd and possibly significant—the world's tallest flagpole. Intrigued and heading in that direction anyway, I stopped in Calipatria for a quick look. Painted white, the flagpole looked like any other except for its long reach into the desert sky. A large plaque below the flagpole informed me it was 184 feet tall. This claim is contentious, I learned later online, and some flagpole enthusiasts (you know who you are) counter that the one in Calipatria—180 feet below sea level and the "lowest down city in the Western Hemisphere" according to the same sign—is merely the world's lowest-lying flagpole.

During my brief trip to the Imperial Valley, I increasingly came to appreciate these quirky, illusory qualities of the desert. The more I looked, or squinted, the more I realized the bone-dry blankness here made it possible to see the landscape for what one wanted it to be, as much as for what it was.

I had been sent south from the state capital in Sacramento to organize a meeting on the once-mighty Salton Sea. Long in decline since its days as a Hollywood hotspot, a little more than a century after its most recent formation, the Salton Sea now blows away in briny clouds of toxic dust laced with chemicals from irrigation runoff.

"An ancient lake remade by a modern mistake," as one writer put it, today's Salton Sea, itself 240 feet below sea level, came to be after land developers constructed a canal to import water from the Colorado River in the early 1900s. The canal silted up, however, so the developers next built ditches and troughs to bypass the blockage. The diversions soon proved all too effective and in 1905 heavy rains overwhelmed the channels and flooded ancient, dry lakebeds known as the Salton Sink. The rush of water from the Colorado River formed a vast landlocked sea thirty-five miles long and fifteen miles wide, and larger than Lake Tahoe. Foreshadowing future efforts to tame the Salton Sea, engineers spent nearly two years repairing the breached waterways, including at one desperate point dumping boulders into the water to belatedly create levees.

At first, the reborn sea thrived and attracted all sorts of wild life of the natural and human kind. Geese, herons, unfortunately named boobies, pelicans and other migratory birds winging by on the Pacific Flyway stopped to feast on fish. People came too, for vacations, for fishing and birding, and for retirement in the sun at new shore-side communities. Resorts popped up and by the 1950s and '60s the Salton Sea became a trendy destination for Rat Packers, the Beach Boys and other celebrities.

But true to its desert surroundings, this high-water mark of the Salton Sea proved to be a mirage. Already in the driest region in California and with few inflows other than excess water from area farms (bringing with it chemicals from pesticides and fertilizers), water to replenish the sea was in increasingly short supply. In the 1930s, the new Hoover Dam limited further flooding from the Colorado River. As the planet warmed due to climate change, extended droughts became common in the Imperial Valley. At the same time, zapped by the cosmic ray gun of the scorching sun, water in the sea continued to evaporate. By the 1980s, the Salton Sea—a terminal lake with no natural outlets—was saltier than the Pacific Ocean and shrinking. Trapped in this briny stew, fish populations dropped precipitously, and birds flocked elsewhere. Resorts faded away, too, along with the water, as once-popular swimming and water-skiing spots turned into mud and sand. Today, roughly thirty square miles of the old shoreline and lakebed are exposed. Toxic dust laced with agricultural chemicals drifts unhealthily over local communities as do odors from the muck. In just over a century since its creation, the Salton Sea went from water abundance to a cautionary tale about water use in the parched American West.

With all this in mind, I arrived on a bright winter morning at an old yacht club near the semi-ghost town and artists' colony of Bombay Beach. The yacht club had recently been transformed into a community center and the rooms converted into a fitness center and an arts and crafts classroom with low kids' tables that doubled as the command center for my meeting. Outside, I stood in a courtyard as state and federal authorities rolled out the latest efforts to help the ailing Salton Sea and reporters took notes. At a podium, officials announced millions of dollars in funding to import water from the nearby New River to create wetlands for fish and birds. The local congressman, Raul Ruiz, spoke of the commitment of the federal government toward these efforts and of the potential for lithium extracted from the mineral-rich lakebed. Conservationists elaborated on the Salton Sea's importance ecologically and even geologically—with the lower volume of water in the modern era (eons ago Salton Basin seas were much larger, and thus heavier) believed to put less stress on the San Andreas Fault far below in ways that could help prevent a major earthquake. In their native language, local Cahuilla leaders spoke evocatively of the importance of the Salton Basin for the Cahuilla spiritually, culturally and historically across thousands of years.

From the courtyard, I could see the beached docks of the old yacht club, now high and dry on brown, reedy ground. Further out, against distant mountains, shards of the Salton Sea shined jewel-like in the sun, a tantalizing reminder of the flush water riches of the past and, just maybe, the water and mineral wealth to come. At the lectern, more officials talked excitedly of this potential salvation, echoing a timeless desert theme of good fortune and destiny just ahead on the horizon.

In the two weekend days I had free after the meeting, I resolved to search for such salvation and ephemeral horizons myself, to see what the desert could teach me about the elusive nature of destinations and arrivals.

After the meeting wrapped up with a buffet lunch spread out on those awkward kids' tables, I drove north past the small town of

Mecca with its long rows of date palms, through similar wind-blown oases with modest streets, churches and family businesses, then headed to more nomadic lands.

I found salvation, of a sort, in Slab City, which was named for leftover concrete pads from its long-ago days as a Marine Corps base. Scattered trailers, recreational vehicles and campers parked on the old pads and blended into the khaki-colored landscape. At the heart of the community sat Salvation Mountain. White adobe, old tires, discarded industrial parts, all formed the dome-shaped mound that was constructed by a local resident in the 1980s. Murals added splashes of bright color, and at the top there was a cross and the messages in red and pink: GOD IS LOVE and LOVE IS UNIVERSAL.

From Salvation Mountain, I moseyed, as much as one could mosey in a rental car, down the road to a nearby lean-to with a wooden board out front and the words "Gift Shop" scratched onto it. I stepped behind beaded curtains into a dirt patio surrounded by rough shelves piled with leather bracelets, polished stones and T-shirts. I selected a shirt reading "SLAB CITY" across the front and in smaller letters along the side, "The Last Free Place," rousting a burly, bearded fellow in cargo shorts and a tank top lounging lizard-like in the sun on a lawn chair out back. Unfortunately, the "last free place" ethos didn't apply to the $15 shirt, and cash was preferred. As the bearded proprietor explained from beneath his straw cowboy hat, even freedom has its costs. I didn't mind, since the black and white shirt neatly encapsulated the laidback, live-and-let-live-spirit of Slab City. Printed on the front were an airstream trailer, an owl, a family of sage hens and an acoustic guitar set against a backdrop of mountains, while fighter jets and a hawk soared in the sky above.

With its knockabout, carefree and creative vibe, Slab City felt like the sort of place where Burning Man devotees might retire. And for those who found Slab City too conventional, I learned from the gift shop guy that further out in the desert was an even more bohemian community called East Jesus.

Since I had a return flight the next day, and not being a Burning Man retiree myself, I decided to skip this far-out holy land and instead visit Joshua Tree National Park.

Continuing to name-check major desert religions as I went, I first stopped at the park's visitor center. Browsing the dioramas and displays, I learned the park was notable for its large number of species that had specifically adapted to the desert landscape. Browsing on, I read that Mormons gave the Joshua tree its name for the way the branches of the yucca plant reminded them of the biblical Joshua reaching toward the heavens. These stumpy, fuzzy branches, seemingly inspired by the trees in a Dr. Seuss book, helped the Joshua tree survive in the austere environment. On the lookout for other similarly desert-adapted creatures, and idly wondering how I might be shapeshifting here myself, I left the visitor's center and followed a serpentine two-lane road for forty miles across the park. In the late afternoon, flowering cactus and Joshua trees moved in and out of shadows while the lowering sun warmed distant, snowy peaks with alpenglow.

At the north end of the park, I stopped for the night at Twentynine Palms. Home to a nearby Marine Corps base, the town's wide streets mixed tumbleweeds and scrub with military barbers, gun stores, surplus equipment outlets, taco stands and tattoo parlors. I checked into a low-slung motel and then walked to a nearby taco restaurant for dinner. Afterward, I strolled through side streets in the early evening chill amid the high desert scents of sage and juniper. As I walked in the vespertine stillness, I found myself recalling snippets of songs from the Irish band U2's album also named *The Joshua Tree*. Back at the motel and tired from the long day, as U2 put it, indeed "Sleep came like a drug in God's country…"

With these lyrics from U2 singer Bono fresh in mind, the next morning I put the *The Joshua Tree* album on Spotify for my drive to Palm Springs Airport. (Also home, I later discovered, to another locally iconic Bono: the late pop star, politician and Salton Sea champion, Sonny Bono, commemorated at the airport by an unsettling, grimacing bronze bust. Sonny, they don't get you, babe.)

As I drove west toward Palm Springs, U2 Bono's words reflected the landscape flowing by: the bullets in the blue sky formed by passing jet planes, one-tree hills, strip malls and small houses on no-name streets, red hill mining towns holding on, blown by the wind and trampled in dust.

Only later, reading Bono's autobiography, would I learn the band had not actually visited Joshua Tree when they recorded the album. Instead, Bono performed his own act of mirage and used the desert landscapes in and around Joshua Tree as a blank canvas to sketch in what he imagined the American West to be.

As for me, passing through the town of Palm Desert, the American West presented itself as big-box stores, oil change "kwik" stops, generic hotels, convenience marts and casinos … "Outside it's America," Bono sang.

I realized, though, I didn't have to stay in *this* America. Summoning the desert powers of mirage and transformation, I instead looked past the chain stores, billboards and highway sprawl and returned to the view of the Salton Sea from the start of my trip. I found myself once again in the courtyard of the old yacht club, the Salton Sea a shimmering blue promise of water even as it ebbed away, for now holding back guttural rumblings from the Earth's crust; the Salton Sea providing final reminders that what you see here in the desert isn't necessarily the same as what lies ahead—or what lies beneath.

A Joshua tree in bloom

Desert Pas de Deux
Cyndi Goddard

In March 2023 on a solo road trip through the high Mojave Desert, I heard Bono's voice. It was soft and lilting, his manner thoughtful as he responded to the hosts of the podcast my personal DJ—Spotify—had spun up for me. It was a prescient selection, given that I was headed to the national park named for the plant Bono had made into an international icon.

To U2 fans, the story of how the singer came to name the band's 1987 album *The Joshua Tree* is legendary.

In December 1986 during a photoshoot in the American Southwest, Bono learned that the Joshua tree got its name from Mormons crossing the desert. Upon hearing that the tree's outstretched limbs reminded the Mormons of the Old Testament prophet with his arms raised in supplication, Bono decided to name the band's latest album *The Joshua Tree*.

When the record was released in March 1987, the back sleeve

featured a black-and-white photograph of the band standing before a lone, twisted Joshua tree in a barren desert. The album sold over 25 million copies worldwide, catapulting the band to international stardom and embedding the desert plant in our communal consciousness.

Hearing Bono speak took me back to November 1987, to the impromptu concert U2 staged one Wednesday afternoon in San Francisco's Financial District. Propelled by rumor and the sound of music bouncing off high-rise towers, a crowd of over 20,000 poured into Justin Herman Plaza, I among them. We were united by, ignited by, the gift of the unexpected. There must have been some pushing as we pressed into the plaza, but I do not remember it that way. I remember the crowd moving as one, energy spiraling up to meet the music, as if we, all of us, were suspended in a moment of perfect synchrony.

I had forgotten that day. In the thirty-six years since, I had become a mother, loved and lost a cherished partner and moved from the city to a small town surrounded by redwoods where I learned to hold my joys and grief in the grace of nature.

"Play *The Joshua Tree*," I said. Spotify obliged and my small car was filled with the anger and the ache of an era. There were songs that spoke of loss and emptiness, open spaces and longing.

Although I felt the sense of isolation and a bareness in the music, around me I was seeing life and renewal. Spring was arriving in the High Mojave.

That winter had brought unprecedented freezes and floods, tree-toppling winds and snow at elevations that had been dry for decades. The conditions that caused chaos for humans and human-built things brought relief to a land that had gone too long with too little precipitation, too few freezes. These conditions were exactly what the Joshua trees needed to bloom.

The haunting "With or Without You" took me through the line at the gate to Joshua Tree National Park. A few miles into the park I lost cell and Spotify coverage but by then I was fully focused on the otherworldly landscape of Lost Horse Valley and its wealth of Joshua trees. Seeing the tall, majestic trees spread across the valley like foot soldiers on the march, my internal soundtrack switched from the melodies of U2 to Ravel's "Bolero," with its driving, martial cadence.

I learned later that the largest Joshua trees in the national park are over forty feet tall and are thought to be more than one hundred fifty years old, and that the trees I was looking at were the *Yucca brevifolia*, which is a separate species from the eastern *Yucca jaegeriana*.

I had planned a hike to Lost Horse Mine for another day. I had not yet done my research, had not bought the books, studied the maps nor talked to the park rangers. That afternoon was to have been a recon mission, but I found I could not stay passively inside my car. I had to get out into the desert landscape, to see the trees and their white clumped blossoms close up. As I climbed a mound of rocks that appeared to have been stacked by a giant, I knew little about the unique biology of the surrounding Joshua trees.

I did not know, for instance, that the plant is not, in fact, a tree. It is a monocot, a member of the asparagus family and closely related to the agave. Since they are not true trees, even the tallest Joshua trees do not form rings as they grow, which means that the only way to estimate a particular plant's age is by its size.

I did not yet appreciate how fortunate I was to be among so many blooming trees. The Joshua only flowers in specific conditions, and it only branches after it flowers. The tall stalks with their iconic uplifted limbs high on the trunk were a testament to warm, rainless winters.

Standing on the towering jumbo rocks, looking out over the valley, I was seeing a brigade that had come of age during drought.

The story that Bono learned was not the only legend about the Mormons in the California desert. Some say it was not Joshua in his guise as prophet that the Mormons saw, but Joshua when he was the warrior leading an invading army.

From my vantage point I could relate to that version of the tale. The trees, like Joshua's warriors, went on and on, marching into the distance, past the rolling hills, beyond the horizon, through history, to a time before humans set foot upon the desert.

Before miners used its limbs as fuel for steam engines, before settlers built fences and corrals from its trunks, the native Cahuilla worked the plant's leaves into baskets and consumed its flowers and seeds. They called it *hunuvat chiy'a* and *humwichawa*.

Humans are not the only animals to feed on the Joshua tree. It is a keystone species. Its branches and leaves create cooler, moister microclimates that shelter desert wildlife from the summer heat. Its fallen leaves provide homes for animals like the desert night lizard. Animals and insects eat its flowers, seeds and fruit. Dozens of bird species nest in its leaves, as do the black beetle and yucca moth. Each of these creatures either feeds or feeds upon others, creating a food web that encompasses the entire desert.

And that web depends upon a relationship unique in the natural world—that between the Joshua tree and the yucca moth. The yucca moth is the Joshua tree's only pollinator, and the moth lays her eggs only on the blossoms of the Joshua tree, and the seeds of the Joshua tree fruit are the only food source of the yucca moth's caterpillars.

Like the Joshua tree, the yucca moth is unique. Unlike other pollinating insects that have long tongues, the yucca moth does not. Instead, it has tentacle-like fronds around its mouth. While almost all pollination is accidental, the yucca moth's is quite purposeful.

The female moth, after mating with the male on the Joshua tree's blossoms, collects the pollen from the flower's anthers and shapes it into a large lump, which she carries under her chin, held in place by those tentacle-fronds. She flies to other Joshua trees, searching for a blossom in the right stage and that has no other eggs. Only when she locates such a plant does she lay her eggs on the flower's seeds. She then goes to the stigma and carefully deposits some of the pollen from under her chin. This ensures that there will be enough fruit to feed her larvae.

Without the yucca moth pollinating it, the Joshua tree would never bear fruit. Without the Joshua tree's flowers, the moth could not reproduce.

The two different species of Joshua trees are pollinated by two distinct yucca moths. *Tegeticula synthetica* pollinates the western Joshua and *T. antithetica* the eastern one. The physiological differences between the two moths precisely match the differences in the blossoms of the two Joshua trees. The distance between the blossoms' stigma and ovule is the same as the difference in body size of the moths. I find the precision of this breathtaking. Scientists call it "symbiosis" and point to it as an example of coevolution.

As my knowledge of the life cycle of the Joshua tree deepened, my internal soundtrack evolved from the raw ache of U2's desert songs through Ravel's militant surge to the complexity of a Tchaikovsky pas de deux. The synchronicity between the Joshua tree and the yucca moth is as awe-inspiring as the greatest ballet. The two are as intimately bound as dancers held aloft by their partners, each dependent on the strength and timing of the other.

This intricate web of connectedness requires not only insect and plant, but weather and climate, just as a ballet needs composers, choreographers and dancers.

I left Lost Horse Valley before nightfall so did not glimpse the flutter of moths around the heavy white blossoms of the Joshua trees. I had to imagine the partners locked in their dance, moving to a melody only they could feel, the pace quickening and the moths responding, adapting, improvising, reaching for each other, their bodies trembling as they strained to remain in sync in an ever-hotter, drier, more crowded world.

A desert garden

Lost Horse Valley
Maw Shein Win

The horse is lost.

Needles from a Joshua tree. Cholla and ocotillo.

Quail, cadet gray.

Moonlit.

Wire-lettuce. Antlion wings.

He passes into the valley.

Left behind: three containers of Quaker Oats, bitter black tea in a cup, empty suitcases tied together with twine. A dusty army cap on the kitchen counter.

The youngest daughter clips his toenails as the monitor slows.

Another daughter flies over the valley.

Roadrunner: *Geococcyx variegata*

A Party on Camelback Mountain
Tom Harrell

He turns heads, but you wouldn't invite him to a party—early some days, late others, a no-show more often than not. There are good days when he lingers, poses coyly, and acts every inch the dream guest.

And then there are the days he eats the other guests.

This is Roadrunner, for lack of a better name. Somehow, just as in the classic Looney Tunes cartoon, *Geococcyx variegata* needs no other moniker, nor do I name my other guests: a daily parade of feathered personalities that, not so long ago, I would have lumped together under the generic label "Birds." Now, I watch the daily soap opera unfold around me.

My house, the stage for this daily ringed gathering, sits just below Camelback Mountain, in the center of Phoenix, which itself sits in the center of the Sonoran Desert. The Mountain is part of the City's Mountain Preserve, a string of mostly urban mountain oases of trails and nature. Because a hugely popular hiking trail runs behind my house, I see few large desert animals other than coyotes. But despite the human crowds—or maybe because of them and the absence of local hungry predators—desert birds flourish.

Hawks and falcons nest in caves and crevices and ride the winds; below, desert quail walk the same paths every day, from dawn to dusk, their feathered scouts ahead and behind, only reluctantly using their wings. Everywhere in this desert landscape hummingbirds, sparrows, finches, doves and cactus wrens feed on and nest in the cactuses and palo verde trees. At night I hear, but rarely see, the great horned owl.

What brought about this new interest in my avian guests? Partly, it springs from sheer numbers. Spring, especially, brings the feathered crowd. At that time the trees, cactuses and native bushes at Camelback Mountain break into startling bloom, a kaleidoscope of yellows, golds, purples, whites, and reds. For a few precious weeks, the vista is stunning. It's hell on allergies, but a visual example, every day, of the genius and beauty of nature.

Partly, I think, my fascination comes with proximity: I'm often outside with the birds, not watching through a window or binoculars. I use those for people, another interesting species. When I sit quietly, coffee or book in hand, unthreatening, life unspools around me. And partly because they are so damn fun to watch.

The finches are playful; the quail sometimes forget they have wings, running back and forth as if trapped by a five-foot fence, finally realizing they can fly; the hummingbirds zip from tree to pool to flower to rest, taking a still respite; and the sparrows, least colorful but most amusing, explore everywhere, turning up their heads to watch me, curious rather than frightened, happy to follow me through the door.

And, just maybe, the spirit of a former first lady lingers on the trail. It was Lady Bird Johnson who helped present the symbolic federal check to local dignitaries in 1968; that finally allowed Phoenix to buy the top three-quarters of Camelback mountain and preserve it for nature. After a celebration and lunch, the first lady declared, "Let's walk up this mountain," and proceeded to do just that—in heels.

Through her actions, and those of countless locals who raised funds by nickels and dimes, an exquisite urban resource was saved. These days, homes cover the lower sides, and a popular trail is crowded almost every day, but the smaller desert animals have adapted.

And birds have adapted exquisitely. Outside the great room stands a mature palo verde, about thirty feet tall, spreading its branches wide. The wild surround makes this my own little Galapagos. As the weather warms, the first hints of buds appear. Soon after, tiny yellow blooms fill the tree and the feast begins. Some finches occupy the top branches, eating the blooms. Others do the same mid-tree. Still others—finches and sparrows—wait below for the falling petals, or graze across the carpet now turning the yard yellow. Why do some eat high, others low? The palo verde is prolific. There is plenty for everyone. Is it a matter of preference? Specialization? Aggression? I still can't tell.

The hummingbirds, too, are active all day. They also enjoy the palo verde blooms, but better prospects abound: flowering agaves and aloes, ornamental bushes with gaudy orange and yellow blossoms, rosemary and lavender planted just for them, purple sage and brittle bush.

Best of all, flying snacks gather above the pool; small insects that provide essential protein. It turns out, to my surprise, that hummingbirds do not live on nectar alone. They are omnivorous, which makes me see the long, beautifully adapted beaks with new respect.

Arizona likes to boast of its "indoor/outdoor" lifestyle, and spring epitomizes that life. Unlike Florida, the dry heat of the desert leaves few bugs to worry about (thank you, hummingbirds?) and the doors can be open all day.

It's the sparrows that make me laugh. They are bold creatures, hopping just a few feet away if I pass by, and pecking about nonchalantly by my feet as I read. They feel quite comfortable—I daresay too much so—sauntering into the house. They seem to think indoor/outdoor living applies equally to them. Unfortunately, my slick porcelain floors mean they slip and slide until they find a rug. I would be more amused if they didn't find things in the rug to eat; that always means it's time to dust off the vacuum. Given the chance, these feathered visitors will fully explore the house, and on those days when I close the sliding doors they give me reproachful looks, as if to say, *What a poor host you are.*

But the good times do not always roll for my avian pals. Predators, from raptors to rattlesnakes, await. Eggs are vulnerable to coyotes and bobcats…and other birds. Even the slow, methodical gila monster, the only venomous lizard native to the United States, is a threat. And, although I hate to say it, so is the roadrunner —my "Roadrunner"—who visits; I suspect because I live on his territorial circuit … and because the birds I love to watch are also his prey.

I watched one day as a sparrow, confident as usual, walked through my yard. Around the corner, Roadrunner looked on. The sparrow jumped. Too late. Roadrunner caught him mid-air and brought him to the ground. In a flurry of hammering beak and flying feathers, he proceeded to eat the sparrow while I observed, mesmerized and horrified.

Sufficient to say, life in the desert is not easy, though peerless mornings and postcard afternoons can make it seem so. The search for food is perpetual, and more than one of my guests has wound up on the plate.

As I write this, temperatures are warming and the desert is on the cusp of renewal. The birds are returning, more every day. Where did they go? Some, like the quail, tread the same path each day, year round. Others, like the finches and hummingbirds, appear to disappear. Something I will have to research.

People often say the desert has no seasons. True, the seasons are more subtle, and guided by the heat, not the cold. But even without the obvious sign—green to brown, to "dead," to green again; rabbits fat and lean and fat again—the extraordinary desert light would tell the tale, the golden refraction just before dusk that transforms anyone, everyone, with an eye or a camera, just for a moment, into Georgia O'Keefe. This is the time of day when my guests are busiest, finding last morsels. The bees, on signal, head into the rapidly falling night. The owls begin to stir and the night things awaken.

There is much for me to learn about my surroundings, and my birds are a start. An unexpected pleasure and company, they have won me over. Forget the white gloves; I have the sparrow test. And this year I will not be embarrassed! Time to open the doors.

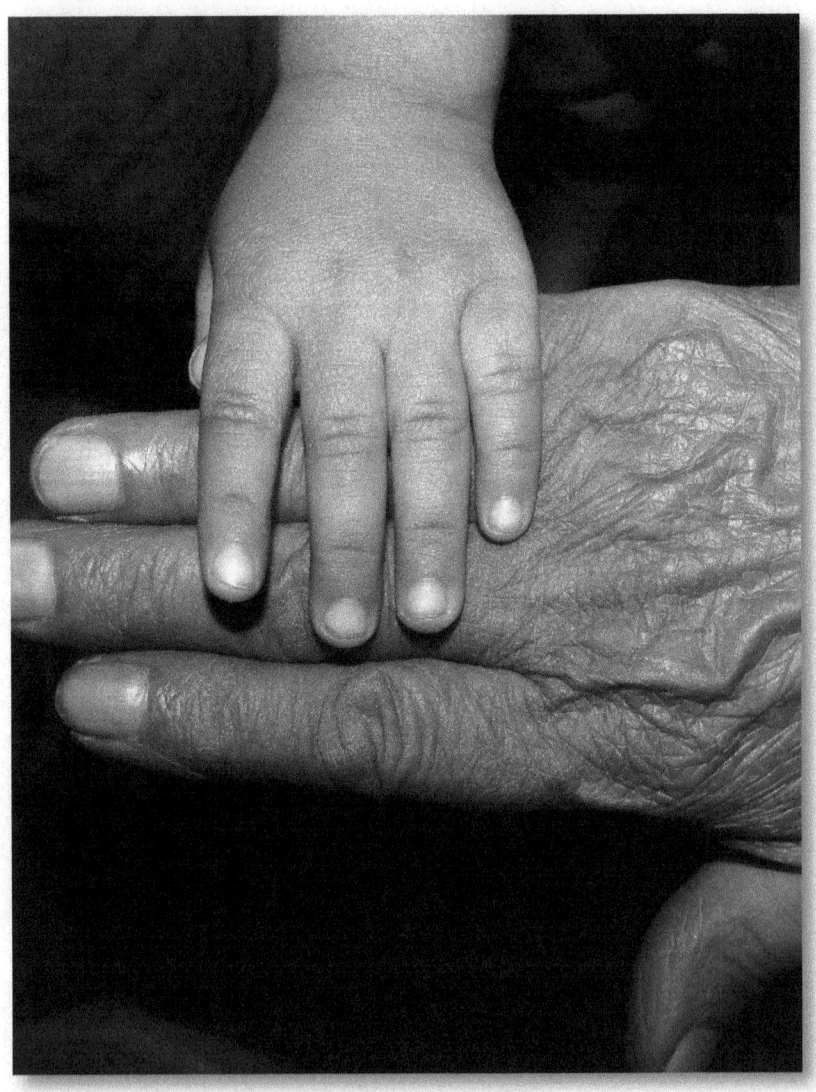

Hands that span the ages

Hands
Maw Shein Win

My father's hands, frail birds, shaking wings.

In Burmese, "win" means bright.

Hands that stitched skin together and brought back life.
Hands that held drinking glasses.
Hands that turned the pages of Hemingway novels.
Hands that prayed for liberation from earth.
Hands that reached for my mother's hand from a hospital bed.
Hand that waved through the bright hot air under a Joshua tree.

goldfinch and *waxwing*

northern flicker

Sedimentary layers of earth upended by seismic activity

Orders of Magnitude
Anne Sigmon

"The shocks and outbursts of earthquakes ... are among the orderly, beauty-making love-beats of Nature's heart."

— John Muir

Like an infatuated neighbor, I've lived and worked in the shadow of California's San Andreas Fault for more than forty years, savoring the Golden State's allure while trying to ignore its perils. And yet, every time the ground rattles or jolts, there's that scary start—breath held, gut clenched—followed by an exhale and a shrug. *Nothing much. Not this time.*

But I also live with the ghost of the monstrous quake of 1906 that killed 13,000 people and left half of San Francisco's population homeless. And I remember all too well October 17, 1989, the deadly Loma Prieta temblor. That day, I braced in a doorway eighteen stories above San Francisco Bay while my office tower jerked like a roller coaster. Not shaking—undulating—the floor grabbing hard for the ceiling. For one awful second, I knew the structure could swallow me.

Memories of that harrowing sky dance remind me that, much

as we'd like to think otherwise, we do not live on solid ground. Instead, we all drift on a set of seven major (and more than a dozen minor) *tectonic "plates"* that have roamed slowly over the Earth's surface for millions of years. These plates are massive, irregularly shaped slabs of solid rock made up of the Earth's crust and upper mantle. The seams where the plates meet—cracks in the Earth's crust—are *fault lines*. North America's grandaddy fault—the longest in the western hemisphere—is the San Andreas, which lurks perilously close to my San Francisco Bay Area home.

The San Andreas Fault marks the boundary between the western edge of California—which clings to the Pacific tectonic plate—and the rest of the state, which rests firmly on the North American plate. When these two slabs bump and grind and slide against one another, they get stuck and pressure builds until—BAM—an earthquake releases energy in waves. Seismic swells collide with unbending rock until the ground shudders. Sometimes it's gentle; other times it's more like Armageddon.

I'd always imagined that the greatest menace from the San Andreas would strike the northern part of the state. But I recently saw a US Geological Survey (USGS) report that astounded me with its forecast that the next "big one" would likely stem from the far south. And it could come at any time—within about thirty years is a pretty good guess.

Such a temblor, the USGS maintains, could ravage California starting with a tremor in what has been dubbed the most dangerous spot in the state: Bombay Beach, a tiny, derelict town perched on a dying lake in California's far southern desert.

The southern San Andreas was essentially a mystery to me, and I wanted to know more. So I enlisted my husband, Jack—ever a science buff—for a road trip south. Armed with a canvas tote stuffed with maps and brochures, geology books, website printouts, binoculars, cameras, and my iPad, we were amateur sleuths setting off to untangle the volatile seismic forces that might well determine California's future.

Our first stop was Palm Springs, about 107 miles east of Los Angeles. A trendy desert resort for decades, Palm Springs is noted for its mid-century modern architecture and natural hot springs. It's also one of the best areas to explore the San Andreas Fault.

Driving into town, we passed miles of dry, dun-colored desert, thousands of whooshing white windmills and a surprising jagged mountain jutting from the flat landscape. That summit, we learned, is San Jacinto Peak, a geologic marvel that, in the course of only seven miles, rockets up more than 10,000 feet. No other mountain in the continental United States rises so high so fast. That meteoric uplift was triggered by the crushing force of two faults—the San Andreas and the nearby San Jacinto. Arrayed on either side, they squeeze the Earth like a vise. Scanning the map, I noticed that the city of Palm Springs was caught in that same trap.

From Palm Springs, Jack and I headed about twenty-five miles southeast to the Indio Hills, an area of arid yellow highlands lifted by the San Andreas. Our destination was Metate Ranch for a guided excursion of the fault zone offered by Red Jeep Tours. The flat, rocky land was parched and pallid under a sapphire sky. There was nothing much to see but some spiney creosote bushes and scraggly Mormon tea grass. I took pictures anyway.

At the ranch, our guide, Darrell, introduced our ride—a vintage, fire-engine-red Jeep Scrambler. Darrell was in his twentieth year guiding desert tours. He looked to be in his forties, weathered by the high sun, a little paunch beginning to form on his fit frame. He was dressed for the harsh terrain with a black sock hat and matching neck gaiter, wraparound sunglasses and a bowie knife sheathed on one hip.

Jack and I clambered into the jeep, and as we rumbled into the hilly maze, I snuggled into my jacket against the morning chill. Soon, we dropped into a flat trough maybe a half mile wide—a bottomland of gray-white sand studded with sagebrush, grasses and the occasional California fan palm.

"It's not hard to spot the fault," Darrell said. If we could view it from the air, for 800 miles, the San Andreas looks like a long valley with little lakes lined up like beads on a strand. The flat valley usually lies snug up against a line of cliffs and ridges. On the valley floor is the *fault gouge*—the pulverized stone found along the fault. The cliffs are the *escarpment*—the rock heaped skyward by the thrust of earthquakes over time. The small lakes are *sag ponds*—pools of water that settle in hollows carved into the Earth when the fault's two plates collide. There is usually a line of vegetation along the base of the scarp cliffs where water pools. In the desert, we find palm trees. Palm Springs, Palm Desert, Thousand Palms—these communities grew up around oases fed by the fault.

"If you think the San Andreas is a defined crack, you'd be wrong," Darrell said. "It's a *fault zone* spanning from ten feet to two miles wide or more." He spoke cordially but deliberately, with the authority of long experience and love of this place.

As our jeep bounced across the valley floor, the trail seemed like something between sand and some kind of fine gravel.

"That's a close guess." Darrell explained that we were riding on fault gouge. That's fine-grained rock material that was ground up by the crushing power of nature when, over millions of years, two sides of the fault bumped and grated against each other.

Just beyond the valley floor, Darrell parked and we hiked up a steep ridge. We crouched on an outcrop surrounded by a moonscape of bare, craggy slopes. Not like the evergreen Northern California mountains I had always loved, but fearsome, naked rock flung up in groaning savagery, again and again, by the slipping and grinding pressure of the two sides of the fault over thousands of years. When I shifted position to regain my balance, a loose stone skittered off into the crevasse.

That's when I realized: The fault is sleeping, right now, beneath my feet. It felt like an uneasy slumber.

"It's never quiet here," Darrell quipped. "We're rocking and rolling all the time!" Indio Hills clocks an average of 292 quakes per year—almost one a day—thankfully, most of them small.

But then I remembered: The monster quake is out there. I shuddered in the afternoon sun.

Earthquakes are classified by magnitude, a number that represents the total energy released by the tremor. According to world-renowned seismologist Dr. Lucy Jones, magnitude is determined by how much rock moves *and* how far it moves. For each whole number increase in magnitude, the seismic energy released increases by about thirty-two times.

The 1906 quake that all but destroyed San Francisco ripped a magnitude 7.8. The USGS's theoretical next "big one" is forecast to be the same—7.8, a fearsome number. Using his earthquake force calculator, Jack reminded me: "That's twenty-two times stronger than the magnitude 6.9 we experienced in 1989." I closed my eyes and tried to pull myself back into my eighteenth-floor office, hanging on, staggering through the sky... then, the newsreels seared in memory of pancaked freeways, collapsed apartments, burning neighborhoods. I tried to imagine it all twenty-two times worse—but I just couldn't.

From Indio, Jack and I steered toward Bombay Beach, population about 250. At 226 feet below sea level, clinging to the edge of the Salton Sea, it's a wreck of a town with an apocalyptic vibe and a sassy attitude. Decrepit trailers, crumbling buildings, wrecked cars and debilitating heat don't dim the village's campy appeal. The place is a temple of quirkiness and deteriorating art installations on a grubby beach: doorways to nowhere, a wooden swing partially submerged in briny water, dozens of decrepit TVs painted in circus colors. Bombay Beach is constantly on the edge of environmental oblivion from receding water, salt scourge, dying fish, punishing heat and the disappearance of wildlife, tourists, jobs and commerce. Earthquakes are just one more in this tiny community's long list of plagues.

But this section of the San Andreas Fault has been pegged by the USGS as the most likely to snap in California's next monster quake. As part of its emergency planning process called the Great Shakeout, the USGS modeled a magnitude 7.8 scenario that ruptures 186 miles of the San Andreas Fault from Bombay Beach to Lake Hughes near Palmdale. Estimates of the damage: more than 1,800 deaths, 50,000 injuries, and $200 billion in damage in areas from Palm Springs all the way to Los Angeles and beyond.

"The springs on the San Andreas system have been wound very, very tight," according to Thomas Jordan, former director of the Southern California Earthquake Center. "The southern San Andreas is locked, loaded and ready to roll."

Bombay Beach might be the projected epicenter, but it was in the Mecca Hills, about thirty miles north, that Jack and I entered the heart of the San Andreas. With no cell bars and spotty GPS, we floundered through fantastical fault geology: a labyrinth of steep canyons, cliffs, crags and outcrops—thrown up and smashed down by twenty-eight million years of tectonic convulsion. We faced bulwarks of rocks, some of them 600 million years old.

As we edged further into the maze, our sedan crawled into a spooky canyon on a road more suited to ATVs than automobiles, skirting mudholes from a recent desert shower. A few curves later, we spun out on sand and got stuck. We were alone in hostile country, surrounded by a frozen tsunami of rock fused in a fury of heat and thrust.

Jack pulled out his pocket compass as we hiked up the canyon. The afternoon sun was low, the sky a bluish purple. Curls, swirls and waves of petrified stone—black, white, tan, gray, brick-red, phantasmagoric green—rose up around us on three sides. Swerves and sideswipes of black-striped rock tilted at forty-five-degree angles.

I stood on the canyon floor. The wind hummed over the stone. At the base of the slope, lit by the slanted sun, I noticed rows of purple lupine and patches of golden poppies blooming on the desert floor.

When I look back on this staggering display, the music of Wagner's *Götterdämmerung* ricochets in my head: In the violin, I hear the crushing tension of seismic waves, in the kettle drums, crashing rocks. The bass is the Earth thundering as stone catapults skyward into new mountains—all of it cacophonous notes of calamity and cataclysm and, finally, creation, as new mountains rise. Then, the trombones signal a return to stasis and the survival of the Earth.

On our journey to the heart of the fault, Jack and I were but specks in the enormity of that fierce country and so vulnerable to the ferocious power that pulsed under our feet. But aren't we all vulnerable all the time? I know that as well as anyone. For more than twenty years, I've lived with a blood-clotting disorder that demands I take dangerously high levels of blood thinner. Travel of any kind is dangerous, and yet I go. It seems to me that earthquakes are no different. Like that explosive blink of the universe, the big bang that started it all, tremors are part of the cycle of life, a continuous loop of destruction and creation.

I had thought of this journey as an exploration. In the end, it became an unexpected pilgrimage—a reminder that, even though we are all at the mercy of the fault, we don't have to live in terror. I'll continue to lean in to California's wild beauty without fear. But with the knowledge I gained in the desert, I'll also let go of ignorance and prepare to survive.

For step one, I vowed to learn more about earthquake preparedness. For anyone who wants to join me, the website Ready.gov is a good place to start: https://www.ready.gov/earthquakes.

"Controlled Thermal Resources looked like the illustration for the cover of a steampunk novel."

Valley of the Future
Cyndi Goddard

"The future happens here first."

When I heard California Governor Gavin Newsom's pronouncement, I thought of a lapel pin I once owned. I had found it in a shop in the Haight in a basket of memorabilia and nicknacks. *No Future.* The stark white letters on black appealed to me, both aesthetically and philosophically. I believed then and still do, that the future, even more than the past, is a construct with no existence outside the mind. I didn't know, when I fastened it to my jeans jacket, that the words were a punk catchphrase made famous by Johnny Rotten and the Sex Pistols.

"Lithium Valley is fast-tracking the world's clean energy future," Governor Newsom said.

It was March 2023. If I had not been traveling in the area, I may not have paid attention to clips of the governor's press conference at Hell's Kitchen in the Imperial Valley, a few miles from the Salton Sea.

I had journeyed to the California desert specifically to see the Salton Sea, and thought I knew all about it. I had read books and articles with statistics about California's largest lake. Thirty-five miles long and fifteen miles wide, the Salton Sea is 226 feet below sea level and just over fifty feet deep. I knew it was a terminal, or landlocked, lake, like the Dead Sea and Utah's Great Salt Lake.

I had perused hydrological and geological studies. I knew the area's origin story—how the Imperial Valley was born in 1901 when the Imperial Land Company built a canal to bring water from the Colorado River to irrigate crops in the dry, fertile soil of the Salton Sink. The irrigation system was considered the largest reclamation project in history and was touted as a shining example of human determination and engineering genius.

The Salton Sea is known as "The Accidental Sea" because it was formed in 1905 when the engineering marvel of the Imperial Canal was overwhelmed by heavy spring rains and flooded. It took two years to stem the breach. In the meantime, farms, homes and businesses were destroyed and the Salton Sink had become the Salton Sea.

Recently, scientists have started challenging the "accidental sea" story. Geological records show that the Salton Sink has flooded and filled repeatedly over millennia. Although the most recent incarnation may have been an accident, the sea is a natural feature.

Whether an accident born of man's hubris or a natural phenomenon that was bound to occur eventually, the Salton Sea has become integral to the Southern California ecosystem. The area is an international flyway for migrating birds and is considered the most important shorebird habitat west of the Rocky Mountains.

Until hearing a sound bite from the press conference Governor Newsom gave after his tour of Controlled Thermal Resources (CTR) in which he spoke of geothermal lithium extraction, I had never spent time thinking about lithium—what it was, where it came from or its integral role in modern life.

As a one-time pysch major, I was aware that lithium was used to treat certain types of mental illness. As a twenty-first century American, I knew that lithium-ion batteries powered my cell phone, laptop and weed whacker, as well as my neighbor's Tesla. I certainly would not have guessed that lithium has sold for up to $70,000 per metric ton or that despite the United States having some of the largest lithium deposits in the world, most extraction occurs in South America, Australia and China. The processes used to produce this key component of clean energy have been destructive to ecosystems, contaminating the soil and air, and diverting resources that local communities depend on.

The Governor had come to the Salton Basin because CTR and two other companies—Berkshire Hathaway Energy and Energy Source Mineral—are pioneering new processes for lithium extraction. All three are developing proprietary technology to filter byproducts—including lithium—from 600-degree brine pumped from the Salton Sea used in geothermal energy generation. Once the lithium is recovered, the brine would be returned deep underground.

If successful, geothermal brine extraction would make California a leading producer of clean, battery-grade lithium. Unfortunately, the process has never been successfully accomplished on a large scale.

Governor Newsom and the state of California are determined to change that. Since 2017 the state has awarded over $27 million to projects researching innovations in lithium recovery and processing, as well as efficient manufacturing of lithium batteries. The goal is to create a clean-energy manufacturing center in the Salton Basin. Lithium Valley would emulate Silicon Valley as a nexus of innovation, financial success and community development.

A sense of wrongness crept over me as I drove south on highway 111 to Bombay Beach on the Salton Sea's northeast shore. I had lived my entire life on one coast or another, never far from the ocean. Oceans and seas belonged on the coast. The sight of all those miles of water stretching to the horizon in the midst of a desert disconcerted me.

I thought I was prepared for the sight of an inland sea. Not only had I read all those articles and books, I had spent evenings on YouTube watching promotional films from the 1960s and '70s. The films portrayed the Salton Sea as a fishing and boating paradise. Southern California families flocked to the sea for frolicking weekend getaways, and water-skiers raved about the speeds they attained on the calm, flat surface and the buoyancy of the lake's high salinity. Celebrities like Frank Sinatra and the Beach Boys used to hang out in the yacht clubs that peppered the sea's shores.

The films showed happy tourists who had been bused in from Los Angeles to walk a grid of streets laid into the sand. The voiceover informed me that sewer and water lines had been installed and, as for power, it came from "...steam wells shooting up from beneath the surface." This geothermal power came from the plants surrounding the sea, plants that might someday serve double duty in the clean energy battle—both for generating power without fossil fuels and extracting battery-grade lithium.

If driving next to a sea in a desert felt wrong, coming across yacht clubs and piers marooned miles from water was downright creepy.

The Salton Sea, like the Great Salt Lake and the Dead Sea, indeed all the world's great landlocked lakes, is drying up. Climate change and the diversion of waters feeding the lakes are contributing to the natural process of evaporation.

I parked on one of the grid streets and hiked toward the water. Remnants of the area's nautical past lay on the exposed playa. First was an anchor, then the broken and abandoned hull of what had once been a sleek speedboat, and next, a series of channel markers rising from the sand.

No, not sand. The white stuff I was crunching under my boots was not sand. It was bone.

The low oxygen and increasingly high salinity of the Salton Sea kills thousands upon thousands of fish every year. Their skeletal remains are exposed as the lake's water retreats. I was fortunate to visit on a calm day. When the wind blows, the sulphury smell of rotting fish permeates nearby communities. Wind across the playa stirs up toxins from algae blooms and pesticides deposited into the lake by run-off from irrigation water. These toxins have become exposed as the sea shrinks. The hospitalization rates for asthma are twice the national average for children who live near the Salton Sea.

When I returned to my hotel room that evening, I pulled up the transcript of the Governor's press conference. Having experienced firsthand how another generation's vision of the future had turned into one of the worst environmental disasters in history, I wanted to believe there is hope for a better, different future for the Salton Sea.

California has been a leader in setting clean-energy transition goals. All new cars sold in the state after 2035 will be EVs. Countries around the world are passing similar regulations. They are closing traditional power plants and setting quotas for clean-energy-powered vehicles. In December 2023, COP28 (the 28th annual United Nations Climate Change Conference) closed with text acknowledging the need to transition away from fossil fuels.

Automobile manufacturers are getting ahead of the laws, providing ever-increasing options for consumers who are ready to give up their gas-powered cars and trucks.

The state's plan not only provides incentives for developing new lithium extraction techniques, it includes the Lithium Extraction Tax. This tax would be used for restoring the wetlands and mitigating some of the damage to the Salton Basin.

Although lithium extraction and the envisioned battery production center could uplift the economy of the entire region, many locals are leery. They point out that the superheated brine contains not only lithium but arsenic, lead and other corrosive substances. Assurances that new extraction technology will keep toxins out of the environment are met with skepticism by those who have heard such promises in the past and have lived through the consequences of accidents, system failures and negligence.

In addition to the Governor's press conference, I pulled up one of the promotional films, listening again to the narrator, who, in archetypal 1960s authoritative fashion, urged me to get in on the ground floor of the "City of the Future." I decided to take his advice and check out Salt City, stopping at CTR on the way. Their department had not responded to my request for a tour but at least I could do a drive-by.

Early the next morning, I filled my water bottles and gas tank, cued up my playlist, and set out for Hell's Kitchen.

CTR looked like the illustration for the cover of a steampunk novel—a collection of smokestacks and block buildings linked by metal ductwork and elbow tubes, all secreted behind chain-link fences. Miles of large-bore pipeline snaked alongside the empty road in both directions.

Staring at the facility from the other side of the entrance gate, I felt its remoteness, the lack of activity in a place that only a few days earlier had hosted the bustle of the Governor's press conference. I walked the dusty road and took snapshots that conveyed neither the desolation of the surroundings nor the scale of the massive power plant.

Driving north on Highway 86, I missed Salton City. If there was a sign, I didn't see it. I did spot the billboard for Salton Sea Beach, another of the past's metropolises of the future, which are now little more than ghost towns inhabited by those too poor to escape the toxic dust, those unwilling to give up the future they once envisioned, and the artists who have found both solitude and community.

Turning off the highway, I bumped along a rutted road, beyond where the pavement ended and past the skeletal remains of a handful of houses clinging to bare, sunbaked lots. Few had intact windows and most of the roofs had collapsed. The remaining paint was peeling and overlaid by graffiti.

I stopped in front of what was once a large, ranch-style house. Most of the walls on the street-facing side were missing, revealing the wooden bones of the building. The single intact wall had been graffitied with large black lettering. The top line read NEW CITY. Below that in crammed-together letters was painted the word COMING. Below that—SOON. The next two lines revealed the date of the new city's appearance and its name: 2023 and LITHIUM CA.

I walked past the houses into the oncoming twilight. As night descended, the empty playa filled with competing futures—the past's future, remade and reimagined by artists and engineers, visionaries and real estate developers; the futures promised by governors and entrepreneurs; the futures being created day-by-day by those who stayed and those who come to enact change.

I realized that the punks and I had it wrong. There's not "No Future." There are many futures. They are always just over the horizon.

The desert grassland whiptail she-lizard is a pretty little thing.

SHE-LIZARDS: SEXUAL RENEGADES OF THE CHIRICAHUA DESERT
Laurie McAndish King

Hidden in remote locations among the towering buttes and high-desert scrub of southeastern Arizona lives a remarkable population of parthenogenetic lizards. For those who haven't memorized the details of rogue reproductive biology, parthenogenesis is the ability of females to reproduce asexually—no males are involved. In fact, these parthenogenetic lizards are *all females*; there is no such thing as a male of the species. I'm intrigued by the idea of such sexual renegades—who wouldn't be?

Biologists have long known that certain invertebrates like bees, wasps and aphids depend on parthenogenesis. Komodo dragons do it regularly though not exclusively; their embryos develop just fine from unfertilized eggs. Crocodiles and several species of sharks resort to it on rare occasions.

The desert grassland whiptail lizard (*Aspidoscelis uniparens*) is famous for her parthenogenetic abilities. She's a pretty little thing, just about five inches long, plus her tail. That tail is beautiful! Slender and a bit longer than the lizard's body, it often lies in a casual-yet-elegant curve as she sunbathes on a rock. In hatchlings it's a particularly fetching bright blue. Her scaly coat is a sophisticated buffy-olive color, and six pale-yellow stripes running down her back—sleek and sporty—emphasize the she-lizard's lithe figure.

All in all, desert whiptails are quite an enchanting species; you can understand why I was eager to see them. One spring I traveled to Arizona's Chiricahua Wilderness Area to have a look.

It wasn't easy to get there. From Northern California you have to drive hundreds of miles south, then cut over and cross Arizona on Interstate 10, exiting at Roadforks, New Mexico. From there you head south and zigzag back into Arizona. Next you take a treacherous, barely-paved road with soft shoulders for quite a ways, continue onto a dirt road, and cross a rugged wash. That last part you can only do in a four-wheel drive.

The name of the place refers to the Chiricahua Apache, nomadic people who lived here and were led by renowned chiefs —Cochise and Geronimo among them. The area is bounded by the Sonoran Desert to the west, the Chihuahuan Desert to the east, and the mountains of northern Mexico on the south. Yuccas and scrubby native grasses dot the landscape. The air is thin; the sun burns hard and bright.

Even the plants have developed adaptations for survival in this harsh climate. The prickly pear cactus, for example, retains water in its fleshy body. Instead of traditional leaves, it has developed sharp spines as protection from marauding animals in search of moisture. Another example: Yucca leaves' waxy coating helps prevent water loss.

Kangaroo rats use a similar survival strategy; their super-oily coats help conserve water. That's just the beginning of their adaptation for desert life, though. These little rodents don't get much of anything to drink, so they effectively recycle their own urine to conserve water. They also have extra-convoluted nasal passages that act as little heat exchangers, cooling their breath so less moisture is lost when they exhale.

Gila monsters and chuckwallas have their own methods: They each store water in fatty lumps—like camels do, except the reptiles' lumps are in their tails. Horned lizards have an intricate system for capturing dewdrops on their body, and spadefoot toads can go into a state of suspended animation for months at a time when food or water is scarce. But as we now know, these feats of desert adaptation are nothing compared with those of the she-lizards.

A quick informational detour is in order here to explain parthenogenesis. I'm not a scientist, but this is what I understand: In certain populations males are absent or in short supply, often for reasons that have to do with habitat availability. So the females just go ahead and lay their eggs without the services of a male or even sperm, and without any of the muss and fuss that typically accompany sexual congress.

Actually, that is not completely true. There is some muss: an unusual chromosomal-triplet-based reproductive method called triploid polyploidy*—a trait the whiptails share with tardigrades and seedless watermelons, and which is too complicated for me to understand.

There also is a bit of fuss: Female whiptails have been observed mounting other female whiptails, in what the scientific literature describes as "female-female courtship and mating rituals." The encounter apparently stimulates ovulation in both participants. At

---

* Because of the way triploid polyploidy works, the offspring would not be *exact* clones of their parents, but they'd be very, very close.

any rate, this almost unbelievable method of reproduction allows a single female to establish an entire new colony, expanding the range of the species.

So if, for example, a roadrunner, which is a predator of the whiptail lizard, were to snatch up a whiptail and fly some distance away with it, but then accidentally drop it, and the whiptail fell, remarkably unharmed, to its freedom in a new-but-whiptail-less land, it would not mean the end of that lizard's genetic line. It would instead be the beginning of a brand new population, and it must have seemed like a splendid evolutionary development ... at first.

But there *is* the matter of genetic diversity. All the genetic mixing involved in "regular" sexual reproduction is why we are each unique, and why our species, made up of diverse individuals, is genetically healthy. The lizards' parthenogenetic reproduction is tough for the community because without diversity it's more susceptible to disease and adverse environmental changes.

It must be tough for the individual lizards, too. Think of it: With no genetic diversity, every lizard would essentially (triploid polyploidy) be a clone of her mother. Same tiny ears, slippery skin, and long toes as her mother had. Not only that, but the mother lizard would be a clone of *her* mother, and so on, back many generations. There'd be little opportunity for variation or evolution—longer tails, keener eyesight, improved camouflage—as would be possible in a population that reproduced sexually.

Imagine what it would be like if we humans had to bear the weight of that endless monotony: identical women stretching out in every direction, even extending backward and forward in time. Mothers, daughters, sisters, aunties, grannies—everywhere you looked, you would see yourself, as though you were living in a hall of mirrors. Glance in one direction and you'd be treated to a vision of your younger self: girlish and fresh. Turn another way and you'd see a specter of your future self: older, slower, wrinklier. Time would dissolve; identity would shift. What would "self" even mean in a colony of clones? In some weird, psychosis-inducing twist you might even glimpse an eternity of universal one-ness. It would be the stuff of nightmares.

This self-cloning behavior seemed to me like more than just a fascinating curiosity of the animal kingdom; it seemed like, potentially, an existentially big deal. Or, at the very least, some kind of cosmic metaphor. At any rate, it's why I really wanted to see the lizards, and why I traveled all the way to a wilderness area and dragged myself through a desert of prickly cholla cactus, yucca and fan palms, punctuated by the occasional Apache pine or netleaf oak, for a glimpse.

The March sky was bright blue, the puffy white clouds picture-perfect, the breezes redolent with juniper and pine sap. My trip was perfectly timed—the whiptails' hibernation season had just ended—so I expected to see loads of them basking in the sunshine, and maybe a few hiding near small seeps or springs, stealthily awaiting their prey.

They are excellent hunters, by the way. Whiptails are so strong they can catch and eat reptiles, mammals and birds that are bigger than they are, when they need to. And they can apparently detect underground predators or prey—from above ground. Interestingly, science has shown that desert whiptails are measurably less aggressive than other lizards. These remarkable creatures are such an enigma! I had a sort of science-crush on them, and could hardly wait to spend quality time hanging out with the whiptails.

At first I didn't see any, so I figured they must all be perfectly camouflaged on the Chiricahua's lichen-encrusted outcroppings. I hiked up higher to have a look. Rocks crumbled into slippery gravel beneath my boots, trails disintegrated and the mile-high air slowed me down, but I kept up my search.

For an entire week.

However, it was unseasonably cool the spring I visited—a full ten degrees below average—and despite my best efforts and all my positive visualizations, the creatures were nowhere to be found. Apparently, they were still underground.

So, I never did get to see a desert whiptail.

But I salute the adaptability, the environmental mastery, the evolutionary ingenuity of these sexual soloists. Cloning themselves in female-only enclaves like Gorgonian immortals, the whiptails have given up genetic diversity in a bid to avoid extinction.

20 Mule Team Borax Wagons

Christmas in Death Valley
Linda Watanabe McFerrin

It was a few days before Christmas. Across the desolate, white-blanketed valley floor, thin lines of visitors trekked wordlessly along. I wanted to reach down and grab a handful of the chalk-colored stuff crunching beneath my boot. I knew, of course, that it was not wet, that it wouldn't compress into snowballs, snowmen or snow angels. Here, the mantle frosting the earth wouldn't melt. The valley floor would never awaken. It wasn't snow enrobing the landscape. We walked on a carpet of chemicals—the salts and borates that perpetually cover the floor of the basin known as Death Valley. Around us the Panamint, Grapevine, Black and Funeral Mountain ranges rose like the walls of an enormous bowl. We were small dots of life making our way across the spectacular salt pan.

We were the runaways, the misfits, people who prefer not to meet expectation in the usual way. Death Valley, at Christmas, suited us perfectly. The desert, after all, supports irony. It deals out jokes like hoodoos and spindly Joshua trees. It's a place for wild asses and sidewinders and empty towns like Skidoo.

Just days before, heading south on 99, my constant travel companion, Lawrence, and I had passed through Bakersfield. Lingering in Kern Canyon, we watched sunlight settle on rock and the Kern River waters. Cottonwood and oak sparkled silver and gold. At noon we arrived at Lake Isabella and stopped close by to visit the Silver City Ghost Town. This was our first real taste of a desert disorientation that shuffles reality like a professional gambler.

The Silver City Ghost Town is a cluster of sun-bleached buildings, each with a rickety provenance, like the old jail that floated up from the bottom of man-made Lake Isabella when it was filled. In addition to the old Isabella Jail, the ghost town is comprised of twenty-six authentic buildings including Wormie Annie's Saloon and the Old Stage Stop. Counting wanted posters, old wash tubs, whiskey bottles, boxes of Hercules gun powder and high explosives, we listened to ghost town creator J. Paul Corlew, or J. C., and sidekick Hal Brown give us lessons in desert history while our noses burned, sweat beaded up on our foreheads and tumbleweeds collected in the center of town.

"White Christmas," "Old Kris Kringle" and "Jingle Bell Rock" twanged from speakers hidden behind the old wooden planks fronting one of those authentic buildings and filled the hot desert air.

*You'll be doing alright with your Christmas of white
while I have a blue, blue Christmas...*

By one o'clock the heat was unbearable. Lawrence and I decided to leave. Hal shook hands with me as we got into the car. He had a horny, hard-working hand. It reminded me of an iguana.

At Walker Pass, elevation 5,000 feet, we entered the California Desert Conservation Area and Ridgecrest, the high desert's "best kept secret," according to the sign. There are lots of secrets in the desert, and the best ones stay that way. We were glad we had four-wheel-drive when we crested the pass, and glad we'd had enough sense to fill up the tank. There wasn't a gas station for miles. The road turned to gravel, and we had it almost to ourselves. One blue car passed us going awfully fast in one direction and came back shortly thereafter going faster. That's how we knew we'd taken a wrong turn. We might otherwise have continued for miles. The desert was already working on us. Experience migrates there, changes like the light. Days drop away like minutes, months like days. Roads lead nowhere, or you end up right where you started and have to start out all over again. We passed the Double Eagle Feed Store and the Cane Break Cafe. We crossed the salt flats between two US Naval weapons centers—scenery minimalist, horizon bare. A chemical smell filled the air. Nothing on the radio—all signals were blocked or scrambled. Searles Lake and Trona, the ugliest town in the world. We slid into Death Valley chasing shadows, low on gas, fueling up our most pressing requirement.

At Stovepipe Wells, we wandered around the small trap of gas pumps and sundry-stacked shelves, with a few other strays, eyes burning inward like a couple of red jasper suns. I saw my first coyote of the trip. I thought it was a yellow dog scooting along, tongue out and trusting cars. It had a mournful look. I think it was begging for food. I knew that coyotes hunted out in the dunes behind Stovepipe Wells. A sign said, "Don't feed the coyotes."

Following 190 past Stovepipe Wells, we were quickly at Furnace Creek Ranch, a collection of buildings that offered unassuming accommodations, a museum, a post office, a restaurant and a general store. Our destination, the fancier Furnace Creek Inn, was visible on a hill to the left. It looked like a desert mirage, an oasis. It boasted a pool, koi ponds, tennis courts, restaurants, gardens and palms. A Christmas tree and a white grand piano dominated the lobby.

"And we thought Liberace was long dead," I observed when we entered.

I was surprised by the number of well-heeled mavericks checking in and out at the front desk. Our reservations had been inadvertently canceled, so Thomas, the manager who was solving everyone's problems that evening, upgraded us to a salmon-colored bungalow that looked out over the desert: Bungalow 100, the last in the line that stretched out along the resort's western face. The room had a fireplace, Victorian fixtures, pale pink walls trimmed in white, chilled champagne in the refrigerator and a view of the Panamint Mountains. Night was coming on, so we headed back down the hill to Furnace Creek Ranch for a buggy ride under the stars.

Mike and Ed, the ranch's two Belgian draft horses, pulled us through the purpling dusk, bobbed tails snapping back and forth on their fat rumps, as we clomped along the roads that crisscrossed the property. Our driver, John, a thin man with a cowboy hat and a tuberculoid cough, identified the few trees we could still see in the gathering darkness—thorny mesquite, feathery blue salt cedar—John told us about bristlecone pine, the oldest tree in the world, about the potash in Trona, and about Dante's View in the Amargosa Range. I asked him about Christmas at the ranch.

"You'd have to wish pretty hard to have a white Christmas here," he laughed. We were moving under a line of salt cedar, the near-full moon peering down on us through the curtain of grey-blue boughs. A bird, a killdeer, flashed past. We rounded the stables. An ass's wild braying filled the night.

"Last night," John said, as if the asses sawing call had triggered a thought, "there was caroling."

I tried to imagine it. Twinkling lights. Night's wet glove. Laughter.

That night it was quiet, our evening nearly unpeopled.

The next day, Christmas Eve, we took John's advice. We headed for Dante's View. It was overcast. We stopped at Zabriskie Point, hiked the rim and descended into the badlands where the yellow earth sprawled, pleated and folded. In that bleached ochre maze, we could hear the low hum of the earth. It was like an enormous generator. The voices of other tourists—an elderly woman's raucous caw, the soft, chocolaty voices of a Mexican family—drifted down toward us in scraps.

At Dante's View, 5,475 feet high in the Amargosa, it was cold. Beneath us a thin dirt road curled like a loose rubber band along the perimeter of the pool of dry white chemical that stretched across Death Valley like a frozen lake.

We took a detour to find and explore a place called Hole in the Wall, a place that didn't exist except perhaps as a spot in a black wall of rock that looked as if it had been riddled by bullets or woodpeckers or termites. We went to 20 Mule Team Canyon, home of the famous Twenty Mule Team that carried borax by the ton to the nearest railhead. The canyon walls were grey, tufted with a white frost-like substance—borax crystals. Heading toward Badwater Basin, the lowest spot in the western hemisphere, we surveyed Devil's Golf Course, then took Artists' Drive to check out the hill known as Artists' Palette—a hillside colored with the verdigris of mica, the yellow-red of iron ore and the magenta and greens of manganese. That day, I remember an exhilarating hike down into the Ubehebe Crater. Seven hundred and fifty feet deep, it was like an enormous natural basket. Carnelian, orchid, jasper and rose-pink walls looked like raffia strands woven together by supernatural hands.

We wanted to go to Scotty's Castle. Like so many desert stories, the history of Scotty's Castle centered around a hoax. In 1906, Death Valley Scotty, aka Walter Scott, persuaded his client, Albert Johnson, to come to the desert and build this spectacular hacienda, a retreat in the middle of nowhere. Johnson was one of many men that Scotty had swindled with his tales of gold mines, but Johnson didn't let that sour their friendship. He considered Scotty's humor and style worth the price he had paid. Scotty never really lived in the castle reputed to be his. He stayed in a small house that Johnson had built for him "just down the road apiece" and acted as property caretaker.

It was a good thing we held off and visited later. Dusk was settling over the desert when we got back to Stovepipe Wells. We scaled the dunes in the twilight, combing them like shell-seekers, only we were reading the stories of kangaroo rats, kit foxes and rabbits written around the entrances of burrows that riddled the dunes' basement dwellings. The golden topaz of sunset turned smoky.

We headed back to the hotel for dinner. As we walked along the veranda, past other bungalow rooms, light filtered through the slats in each room's wooden shutters. A warm breeze floated up, teased the diaphanous draperies of one of them. They fluttered inward. My eye followed their movement, and I saw through the windows, the posterior parts of a large man recumbent upon the nude form of a woman. He covered her completely except for one of her braceleted brown wrists that had escaped the all-encompassing envelope of his hefty embrace. The naked man was shell-pink, a rhodolite brilliance flushing his backside and thighs. I felt a purely aesthetic pleasure in the vitality of flesh stir within me. Wasn't this, after all, a kind of nativity scene? They lay there in bed, a strange bipartite creature, their every breath cooling the man's sweaty withers. To the right, under starlight, the desert was winking towards indigo. I nudged Lawrence, who looked through the window, frowned, grabbed my arm and pulled me along. I couldn't shake the image from my mind. At dinner, as fellow diners arrived, I searched for those familiar parts. I would know the couple only by the man's generous haunches. It proved impossible to recognize them, although I thought I had found him once or twice.

We sat at our window seats looking out. The desert, now dark, was feathered in silhouette—cloud, palm, distant mountain. Waiters moved dreamily from table to table serving excellent food and rendering uneven service. I was enjoying the incongruity of champagne sorbet, sea bass and jumbo prawns in Death Valley. We were epicures adrift in the desert, making our own reality. This reality had something to do with good food, true feeling and flesh.

In the dining room, Santa and Mrs. Claus were making the rounds, visiting tables, stopping now and then to wish guests a merry, if slightly irreverent, Christmas.

Zeroing in on me, Santa approached.

"Have you been a good little girl?" he asked with a wink.

Remembering my pre-dinner amble, considering our escape from familial obligation and our indulgence in personal pleasure, I decided to opt for the truth.

"Oh no, Santa," I said stridently, grateful for our escape in this responsible season. "I've been bad. Very bad."

"Ho, ho, ho." The desert-rat Santa beamed. "Very Good. Very

good." His words were like a pat on the knee. Then he turned to Lawrence. "You hear that?" he asked. "Buy her a fur coat!"

"Maybe after we leave the desert," Lawrence quipped wryly. "What a Santa," he whispered as Mrs. Claus whisked her partner away.

"A fur coat in Death Valley," I marveled. "That seems so peculiar."

"Yes," Lawrence agreed. "But then, so are we. Besides, we've seen stranger things."

A museum poster of Tribal Leader John R. Preckwinkle III with an artifact from his ancestral people.

Finding Cahuilla
Madeleine Adkins

I'm killing time in the Tahquitz Canyon Visitor Center when I realize I've missed a call ... the call for my Cahuilla interview.

The Cahuilla language, also known as *Ivilyuat*, is the original language of the Palm Springs area. An Uto-Aztecan language, it's related to many languages of the western United States and Mexico. I'd asked the local Cahuilla community, known as the Agua Caliente Band of the Cahuilla Indians, if I could interview people involved with the language and its revitalization. I've been waiting, hoping they'd say yes.

I look down at my phone and see a missed call and a voicemail message from an unknown local number. The caller says his name is John R. Preckwinkle III, and he's a tribal leader. I'd been told I'd only be able to interview one person; this is apparently that person.

The message says his council meeting just ended. He's free for an interview now at the Tribe's administration building and has to leave soon. Can I meet him there? I head out to my car.

The administration building is on the other side of town, so I make my way there as fast as I can. As I look at the landscape and the buildings I pass by, I wonder how it looked before Europeans arrived, back when the Cahuilla people lived all across this desert land. The surrounding hills—filled with cactus, rocks and not much else—look as if they haven't changed over the centuries. But of course, the city of Palm Springs would have looked quite different. It's now mostly a pancake-flat grid, interrupted by the occasional flood channel. And the city has evolved into a much-vaunted paean to mid-century modern architecture with low-lying houses, hotels and shops filling up much of the grid. And apart from a few signs I saw in the middle of town, I haven't noticed much that might be in the Cahuilla language. The lack of Cahuilla words around town isn't really surprising—in California, the Indigenous history of any given town or city is usually invisible or difficult to identify. Few places have recognizably Indigenous names. And few structures from California's Indigenous past still stand—a recent hot topic has been the San Francisco Bay Area's four hundred or so shell mounds razed in the nineteenth and twentieth centuries to make way for dance halls, stores, office buildings and highways. California's Spanish heritage is, in contrast, difficult to miss. Especially in coastal spots such as San Francisco, Santa Barbara and San Diego, where everything from the city's names to certain street names, to their eighteenth-century mission buildings are popular tourist attractions that every California child learns about in fourth grade.

Twenty minutes later, I arrive at the Tribe's headquarters, where a receptionist invites me to take a seat. Awards, photos, art and news articles line the shelves along the walls. I find a picture of the current elected leaders of the Agua Caliente Band, including John.

While I'm waiting, I google John's name to see what I can find out about him. Up pops an article calling him a "bird singer." I have no idea what that is and make a note to ask. As I begin reading the article, my contact arrives and whisks me off to the second floor conference room.

John arrives a few minutes later, in a suit, as the council members all are in the photo. We shake hands and take our seats. John begins by giving me an overview of the Cahuilla language situation and the various programs the Tribe organizes to keep it alive and encourage people to learn to speak it.

Whereas in the late 1950s a quarter of the Cahuilla population spoke the language, now only a handful of fluent Cahuilla speakers remain. Unfortunately, this kind of loss has happened to many Native American languages. In some tribes, there are no speakers left, and the language is dormant. Some languages have only minimal documentation. So, Cahuilla, which has speakers and some early twentieth-century recordings and other documentation, is in relatively good shape. But it's still highly endangered.

In the past, the US government did its best to eliminate Native American languages along with traditional cultural practices. In some areas, including here in Riverside County, boarding schools were set up to "take the Indian out" of children by removing them from their families and communities and raising them in an academic environment that focused on the dominant culture's values, religion and, of course, language—English. In the 1950s, it was illegal for Native people to speak their languages in these boarding schools and transmission to the next generation was discouraged. Cultural practices and languages had to go underground if they were to survive at all, and much was lost during this period. As a result, many Native languages were not passed on to the younger generations. Similar events took place around the world—as nations began public education systems, they often required that teaching and learning be done in the official national language. The result was that many local dialects and Indigenous languages lost many (or all) speakers. Of the seven thousand or so languages that currently exist in the world, more than half, and perhaps as much as ninety percent, could be wiped out.

It was only in the '60s, '70s and '80s that traditional and Indigenous cultures around the world began being celebrated. Language revitalization programs were founded in some communities. This renewed appreciation for traditional languages and cultures was inspired by communities' cultural pride, a greater understanding of the value of diversity, and an understanding that something important was in danger of being lost if efforts weren't made to celebrate and pass on traditional culture, language and practices.

There are many reasons that communities have been actively revitalizing their languages. Community members want to be able to speak their own languages again, they want to feel a deeper connection to community, traditional forms of storytelling, traditional practices (such as songs and rituals), traditional knowledge and worldviews. Another reason for this reappraisal is that there's more and more understanding that a community's language is a key part of cultural identity—both for the community and for its individual members. For the past fifty years, communities have been fighting to recover, save and pass on their languages and dialects to younger generations. As culture- and language-erasing policies have given way to an era of cultural and linguistic celebration, minority and Indigenous communities have been working as fast and as hard as they can to save their languages, with the clock ticking. Passing on cultural heritage means uncovering, preserving and teaching traditions to the younger generation. Passing on a language can be much trickier and involves a great deal of time and money. Are there any living speakers? Any recordings, grammars or dictionaries available? Even when there are linguistic resources and fluent speakers, as is the case for Cahuilla, it's not easy. Anyone who's taken a couple of years of high school foreign language knows that studying something for a few years doesn't guarantee that you can speak it comfortably—never mind fluently.

John, as both a current member of the Agua Caliente tribal council and the former chair of the Tribe's cultural committee, gives me an overview of the Tribe's language revitalization work. One key program that the Agua Caliente Tribe has set up is a version of a "master/apprentice program" to pass the language on to select members of the younger generation. In the Tribe's program, a fluent speaker is paired with up to four non-speakers. This is not a classroom-learning approach. Instead, it mimics traditional family interaction and language transmission to the next generation. The older, fluent speaker and the apprentices work closely together, doing everyday tasks, twenty hours a week, using the language while they interact. These programs work well in communities with very few fluent speakers—precisely because they don't require them to be teachers.

Not every community can support this type of language-learning program, as it's time-intensive. The Agua Caliente Tribe is able to do that, even if only on a limited scale—there's currently one student in this intensive program. John speaks about the deaths, in the past few years, of elderly fluent speakers. When only a handful of fluent speakers remain, every time one dies, their particular knowledge of the language is gone with them.

John also describes the weekly language classes offered to tribal members. Adult tribal members can attend the classes as much as they want, and teens are allowed if they're accompanied by an adult. The combination of the master/apprentice program and these weekly classes means that more and more people within the Agua Caliente community are beginning to speak the language every year. But the numbers are still small.

He also tells me about the Tribe's efforts to share their language with the broader Palm Springs community. Native American communities can be very protective of their languages, given how their languages were suppressed by the US government and treated as objects of curiosity by non-Indigenous researchers in the past. So it's remarkable that the Agua Caliente have decided to share their language and culture.

One example John gives is a local Cahuilla artist, Gerald Clarke. To engage the broader Palm Springs community, Clarke has planted signs with Cahuilla words around town, John adds that the name of the new spa that the Tribe is opening, *Séc-he*, is the Cahuilla word for the sound of boiling water.

Moreover, the Tribe has created an award-winning three-year curriculum that introduces the Cahuilla language and culture to children in the Palm Springs schools. Every child who goes to public school here—regardless of heritage—is introduced to the area's original language. An amazing gift. What if we all had that opportunity? To learn the language of our ancestors? To learn the original language of our local area?

I think back to my own experience, growing up in Northern California. There was no push to teach us the language of the Ohlone, the people who've lived in the Bay Area for thousands of years. There wasn't a mention of it, or them, in my classes.

Many of us born in the United States do not have close ties to the languages of our ancestors whose native tongues often linked them to painful pasts. They put aside their original languages, along with their memories of the old country, their customs, their recipes and their religions. Having grown up with no Jewish traditions or culture, I decided, in my early thirties, to reconnect with my Jewish heritage. I knew that my mother's family was Jewish, but I didn't have any idea what that meant. Part of that process was learning traditional and newer prayers and songs in Hebrew. I took a few Hebrew language courses, as well, so the words I intoned would be more to me than mysterious syllables. To my surprise, I felt a profound sense of connection to my ancestors while singing traditional prayers. By participating in these ancient rituals, I was adding my voice to thousands of generations who sang these exact same prayers and blessings, as if we were all chanting together, across time and space.

Then, in 2000, I traveled to Ireland for the first time to connect with that part of my heritage. I took Irish language courses for a few weeks at a summer school in a remote corner of the island, where the language is still spoken. The many ways that Irish is different from English intrigued me—the spelling system, the mutations, and so much of the grammar. But what was particularly interesting to me was that some of these differences express a different worldview. So much of culture is embedded in language; it's part of how we experience and talk about the world every day, and we take it for granted.

Learning Irish had stirred something primordial in me, as if I'd heard these words and experienced these conversations in another time. I felt a sense of home as I spoke in Irish. With Irish, as with Hebrew, it was as if I was finding a part of myself—one that had been hidden in the cobwebs of the past.

I ask John about his own experience with the Cahuilla language. Was he one of the lucky ones who grew up immersed in the language and culture of his people? I knew, after all, of his being involved with something called "bird song"—something very important to the traditions of the Cahuilla.

John explains that he grew up in a small town in Northern California, far from Palm Springs. A Native American in a very White community, he felt different from those around him. And while he knew he was Cahuilla, he didn't know anything about his peoples' history or traditions, and he knew none of the language. His friends would ask him about his culture, and he had no answers. He felt ashamed of his lack of knowledge.

That all changed when he was fourteen. On Christmas Day, he opened a present from the Cahuilla Tribe—a gift that was sent out to all members. It was a CD filled with Cahuilla language lessons and bird songs, the traditional narrative songs of the Cahuilla people. Thirsty for this knowledge, he dove right in, spending hours and hours listening to the CD and practicing the language and the songs.

As soon as John was an adult, he made his way to the Palm Springs area and became an active member of the Tribe, joining the cultural preservation committee and a bird song group.

John worked hard to learn more and more songs. Learning bird songs is a major undertaking, as these are songs that tell stories of the Cahuilla migration and traditionally would be sung beginning at sundown for multiple days. Eventually, he became a head bird singer—a very important role, as bird songs are only allowed to be sung when there's a head singer present.

Bird songs were banned in the 1950s in the United States. The Cahuilla managed to preserve the songs, but the practice had to go underground. Communal bird song events were held in secret, so they couldn't be detected by authorities. Nowadays, Cahuilla bird singers proudly sing their songs in their community—and with the wider world.

John turns to me and asks if I'd like to hear a bird song. Yes, I say, thinking he'll play a recording for me. Instead, he offers to sing and let me record. His song is short, and he explains the words to me, while accompanying himself with a traditional percussive instrument. He sings with a clear voice and powerful timbre. I thank him for letting me record his singing and turn off my recording app. Then he sings a few more songs—I'm being gifted a mini-concert. Listening to the songs, I close my eyes. I can't understand the words, but I find myself imagining the earlier times of the Agua Caliente Cahuilla people in Palm Springs—before the Europeans, before the grid streets, before the midcentury modern houses, before the tourists and before this little valley became a city.

Then John tells me a story. When he learned the bird songs from the CD when he was a teenager—those songs that first connected him to his community, his culture, his language—he didn't know anything about the singer on the recordings. All he knew is that they were copied from wax cylinder recordings made in the early twentieth century. Years later, he found out more about those original recordings. The voice he'd first learned bird songs from, the man who'd first inspired him, was his great-grandfather. His own ancestor had been able to pass on his songs and traditions to John, a great-grandson eager to learn about his culture and language, many decades and hundreds of miles away. And now the little boy who grew up so far from the Cahuilla, so far from his culture and language, is a man who has become a leader of his people, passing on the traditions, the language and the songs to the next generation.

Image of a Cahuilla woman, "The Harvester," from *The North American Indian* by Edward S. Curtis. Original photogravure published in 1924.

The Girl Who Swallowed Words
Joanna Biggar

She was the girl born in Los Coyotes, where the mountains soared, so she spoke Mountain. She was the girl who moved to Morongo, so she learned Pass. When Grandmother moved into the house with eleven children, she learned Desert. She was the girl who knew all the tongues of *Ivilyuat* (Cahuilla), who devoured the words, who loved them. At the White school, she was the girl who learned White words and swallowed them, too. She was the girl who ran with the boys, who wrestled the wind, who told the man to take down his sign, "Whites Only," at the restaurant. He did.

She was the girl who became the teen who studied the plants and loved them. The teen who followed the Medicine Woman, her mother, and learned which ones healed, which ones poisoned. She was the teen who understood how each plant was wrapped in its own word, and how the words and the plants together formed the world for her people to live in.

She was the teen who became the woman who spread her Cahuilla words, her songs, her voices of birds, her prayers, and cried when she knew nobody could hear them. Nobody could hear them because nobody had taught the children. Wrapped in the fury of the wind, she was the woman who became the teacher, teaching the words, the songs, the plants and their powers to children, to adults, to foreigners. She was the woman who knew all the words and wrote them on paper white as snowflakes that drifted from the mountains. Folk tales, dictionaries, stories of plants, the stories of her own life. Objects, books, words, living things all saved in the Museum named *Malki*.

She was the woman who became the elder the world loved to praise.

Now she is the ancestor who blesses her people. You might want to find her in the gardens at Morongo, beneath the mesquite and oak, among the acorns, cactus and screw beans. You might conjure her warm face and dark eyes beneath a ring of white hair and the brim of a hat where all the figures are dancing. When the wind whirls and the sand whips your hair, you might think she is coming. You will not see her, but you will see what she has created and what she still has to teach you. Surely beneath the wind you will hear her; she will be reading softly, so you must listen with your heart. It is her story, *Isill Héqwash Wáxish: A Dried Coyote's Tail.*

Editor's Note: Dr. Katherine Siva Sobel, a member of the Agua Caliente Band of Cahuilla and co-founder of the Malki Museum in Morongo, resided on the Morongo Reservation near Palm Springs, where she died in 2011 at 91. A pioneer who worked to save her language and culture, she became a nationally renowned activist, educator and ethnobotanist whose many honors included being named the California Elder of the Year in 1987, and inducted into Women's National Hall of Fame in 1993.

VISIONS

Salvation Mountain love story

Salvation Mountain, A Love Story
Joanna Biggar

More than a two-mile ride down a dusty desert road from the little town of Niland east of the Salton Sea, a vision, improbable as a mirage, suddenly appeared on the bleached sand. A fifty-foot peak called Salvation Mountain, a mosaic of waterfalls, flowers, Bible references and a large red heart, all painted in shiny red, green, white, blue and yellow, jutted into the uncluttered sky.

Atop the mountain sat a large cross, and below the cross huge red and pink letters proclaimed "God is Love." If the mountain's creator had been asked to sum up his life in one phrase, that would be it.

It was 1996 and I was a reporter who had come, along with a photographer, on assignment from a D.C.-based wire service, to uncover many of the exotic life forms, including human, in the expansive Southern California deserts. Leonard Knight, 64, qualified as one of them, and appeared to be even more improbable than his remarkable creation. He invited me to sit with him in his "living room" on a broken-down couch—its sole piece of furniture—beneath the scanty shade of a mesquite tree, the wide blue sky its ceiling, the sand beneath our feet its floor. We commenced one of the most memorable interviews of my career.

Like ancient prophets who went into biblical deserts to find their visions, Leonard had come to this desert eleven years before to find his calling as an artist. With his lithe, boyish frame, a smile of innocent sweetness, beardless and with hair the color of desert sand, he did not seem quite prophet nor artist. In song, he called himself a "hobo bum." But to me he seemed more a reborn version of the Little Prince, or a variation of that American original, Johnny Appleseed, spreading seeds of love.

"I never was an artist," Leonard said, Yankee grit from his native Vermont still lacing his speech. "Least I don't think so, but the museum people seem to think so, so I'm going along with it," he explained with a nod to the recognition his work had suddenly gained. It had been compared to Watts Towers, the famed Los Angeles monument of metal, glass, shells and junk completed over thirty years by artist Simon Rodia. Articles began appearing; Los Angeles critic Larry Yust had completed a book and a documentary about Leonard's work; the Smithsonian had visited, CNN had run a story.

All this was simply astonishing to the self-described jack-of-all-trades whose previous jobs included painting cars and changing eighteen-wheeler truck tires in Arizona. But, he explained to me, all that changed and his life turned around in 1967, the year he let Jesus into his heart. Although he never belonged to any church, a strict interpretation of the Scriptures became Leonard's guiding light.

"I used to criticize my sister because she talked about Jesus a lot," he said. "I thought I didn't need Jesus, but I guess I did." That was Leonard's explanation, and his confession.

A big part of Leonard's conversion meant repenting of his sins, which he told me included using bad language and having a grumpy attitude. But the biggest part meant feeling a call to speak of God's love. His first method of trying to spread the word was by means of a hot air balloon. But the challenge of getting the thing to fly first took him to San Diego, where it failed, then to Shelton, Nebraska, where his truck broke down. He meant to stay there only two hours—enough to get the truck repaired—but he made a friend. Harold Jones encouraged his endeavors, so Leonard stayed five years.

"Harold's wife loaned me a sewing machine to sew up the balloon," he explained. "I tried repeatedly to get it up. Folks told me it was too big."

They were right. Leonard made one last effort near Slab City, a razed Marine base where trailers park in the winter. But it was too late.

"After sixteen years, all I had was a rotted-out balloon, and I felt like saying, 'God, I'm not doing too good.'" He admitted embarrassing discouragement, but not defeat.

Instead, it came to him to paint the high sandbar nearby. He began with the huge red heart in the middle of Salvation Mountain. At first he shored the sandbar up with cement, "but after three years," he said, "it fell down. So I began rebuilding with adobe." The sand, mixed with water he carried in plastic containers on his bicycle, turned hard in the baking sun. It was further strengthened by twigs, marbles, putty and other objects he added. It was also strengthened by the paint.

Once people learned about the mountain, they began donating paint to Leonard. The state of California (which owns the land) contributed gallons of the yellow paint normally used for painting the lines on roads. That lead-based paint, in particular, led to denunciations that began a few years later by environmentalists, who called the mountain an "environmental nightmare" and wanted to tear it down. As with other adversities, Leonard surmounted that one and said he didn't like to dwell on it.

In fact, he told me, he "was happier than anyone you've ever seen" in his private Eden. And I believed him. For me, however, sitting in the dizzying sun and hardly protected by the skinny mesquite tree, it was slightly less than idyllic. Especially when Leonard began describing the amenities of his daily life: living in a wildly painted truck, bathing in a nearby mineral hot spring, having an occasional coffee break with friends in town. Despite being a loner, he insisted he was not lonely. In fact, he said he was still looking for a wife. When he suggested it might be me, I could only politely decline and privately conclude this was not only one of the strangest interviews I had ever conducted, it was hands down the strangest proposal I had ever received. And I tried desperately not to swoon from the unrelenting sun, figuring he might take it the wrong way.

Still, Leonard's message, large enough to embrace the whole world, endures. "The world needs a good love story," he said.

I filed my story about Leonard in 1996. In 2011, Leonard entered a long-term care facility in El Cajon, for dementia. Meanwhile, due to harsh sun and desert conditions, concern for the upkeep and care of Salvation Mountain, which continued to attract hundreds of visitors, grew. A public charity, Salvation Mountain, Inc., was established to maintain it, and in 2013, the Annenberg Foundation contributed $32,000 to improve its security. Over the years, the project has continued to garner accolades from celebrities, politicians and critics; it was referenced in Sean Penn's 2007 film *Into the Wild*; articles, including one in the

National Geographic, interviews and entire books about it proliferated; and it has become an officially recognized national folk-art treasure.

Leonard died in 2014, at age 82. His dearest wish, however, still stands in the desert—his mountain proclaiming "God is Love" remains for all to see.

The Wizard of East Jesus

The Wizard of East Jesus
Laurie McAndish King

"You have to look for me to find me."

East Jesus is not an easy place to get to. It's in Southern California, off the southeast side of the Salton Sea—the opposite side from Palm Springs. The unpopulated side. Highway 111 takes you to the turnoff at Niland, which leads you over to Slab City, and then you're almost there.

Slab City, also known as "The Last Free Place," is a rent-free, plumbing-free, power-grid-free, trash-pickup-free jumble of ramshackle structures where a US military training facility once stood. The government dismantled its site back in the 1950s, removing pretty much everything but a raft of concrete slabs, which formed the basis of the current encampment. It's a haven for the impoverished and indigent, for off-the-grid artists and the photographers who follow them.

A dusty, rutted road leads out the back of Slab City and curves around to the left, delivering visitors to a small parking area where a sign designates the "En-Trance" to East Jesus. And *entrance* you it will. At first the place looks like a junkyard, with old cars and random pieces of detritus strewn about. But stroll through the sandy pathways of East Jesus and an odd kind of order emerges. The desert junkyard morphs, on its own schedule, into an outdoor art gallery—an art yard—as viewers take in more and more of the elaborate detail, the clever assemblages, the creativity that has blossomed here.

I'd visited other art installations in the area—Noah Purifoy's found art near Joshua Tree; the eerie, sand-swept installations at Bombay Beach; the 100+ gigantic rusted-steel dinosaurs at Galleta Meadows. But East Jesus excites my imagination the most.

Named because it's so isolated, rather than for any religious reason, this "experimental, sustainable, habitable art installation" is technically a museum "interested in low-tech solutions, unresolved theories, non-linear advancement, and creative reuse." The community also seeks to inspire people to see beyond what something is, and instead see what it can be. I'm eager check it out.

When I arrive in East Jesus the first time, at ten o'clock on a June morning, a hot breeze is already blowing. I am immediately overwhelmed by the view from the parking area: a rusty swing set with automobile seats hanging precariously from its bent crosspiece, a motorboat with an airplane propeller at the bow, a mannequin sporting robot arms and a gas mask, harvested circuit boards, painted tractor tires, bowling balls.

A makeshift canopy near the entrance throws off a small shadow. Beneath it, a man with a big belly, a long white beard, and a curved long-stemmed pipe sits on a chair in the shade. From a distance, he looks so much like Santa Claus that for a moment I have the idea this is where Santa comes to warm his bones during the off season, but then I realize that doesn't make any sense. Maybe the desert heat is getting to me. This man is wearing a fluorescent orange East Jesus T-shirt that reflects upward to give his face an eerie, un-Santa-like glow. Also, he has a yin/yang tattoo the size of a quarter in the middle of his forehead.

I approach cautiously.

"Hi, I'm Laurie. Do you live here?"

"I do." He nods.

"What's your name?"

"They call me the Wizard."

Not Santa, then. That clears things up. The Wizard invites me to sit down, and we chat for quite a while about *Marvin the Martian Looney Tunes*, the Wizard's memories of his various churchwarden pipes ("each one is unique, and to be cherished"), and social evolution ("mutate or die"). He mentions his estranged son, but when I ask what his son thinks of this lifestyle, the Wizard clams up. For a minute I think he might cry, but his eyes remain dry.

We are in the desert.

The Wizard has lived in East Jesus for more than a decade, almost since the inception of the community. "I'm an amateur sociologist," he says. "I've watched East Jesus and Slab City grow and dance around, trying to form a community without rules. There lies an inverse relationship between freedom and security. The more you have of one, the less you have of the other." *Yes*, I think. *That's part of why I came to the desert—to escape the security of my daily life, to taste the real freedom that comes with insecurity. But now that I see what life is like here, I'm not sure I'm up for more than a quick visit.*

"Slab City was here first, then East Jesus came about, then Bombay Beach is most recent," the Wizard continues. "It's the most vibrant; it's getting all the big money... Oh! Oh!" he interrupts himself excitedly with an idea that just can't wait. "And my favorite, my very favorite, is the twelve-foot seesaw." He points to a gigantic seesaw that until now had been overshadowed by the boat and the swing set and the masked mannequin. "I am the creator of one thing here. I held it all up with bowling pins, put some rebar in and some glue in. I was at the top of my game there." He laughs.

The East Jesus seesaw really is twelve feet tall. It consists of one very long board balanced on a neatly welded steel frame. Rusted bicycle seats are attached at each end, and the handles seem to be made from old saw blades. The contraption looks impossible to ride, but the Wizard tells me it can be done, although it takes three people to maneuver two riders onto the seats. "It's like the first time," he says. "Remember when the seesaw was twice as tall as you were? It still is!"

The Wizard pauses, perhaps assessing my vibe. "Are you familiar with term power vortex? Some people have a desire, a compulsion, a *force*—call it what it is!—to create art."

"A lot of them seem to have ended up around here," I observe. "Is there much interaction between these artist communities—Bombay Beach and Slab City and East Jesus?"

"We know each other very well, but interaction, no. They're a bunch of artists. They have these things called egos; there are different groups, camps." Another part of the reason the residents didn't talk to outsiders was that they didn't want to invite company. "Unless it was someone you wanted to live real close with for a long time," he continues. "No one talked about Slab City. No one talked about anything."

I'm honored that the Wizard is talking to me now. He doesn't seem to have anything else to do—nothing that's pressing, anyway—but still, it's nice that he's sharing his time with me, telling me about the history of the area, introducing me to art-yard highlights. This must be what all his days are like, talking with visitors who have come to take in the spectacle that is East Jesus. Some are doubtless Green Day fans, here to pay homage to the band's 2009 anthem "East Jesus Nowhere."

Some have come specifically to see the TV Wall. East Jesus' best known installation was constructed from more than one hundred scavenged televisions and computer monitors. Each screen displays a hand-painted message: *Better Living through Sedentary Obedience. Insecurity We Trust. You Need More Stuff. You have the Wrong Opinion. White People Yelling at Each Other. Turn Me On. Dear God No.* The official description calls it "a castrated pile of technology," and says the TV wall will remain a work in progress as long as there's room to keep adding on, either horizontally or vertically.

"What do you do here all day?" I ask.

The Wizard pauses again. He pulls a hefty pinch of tobacco from the canister that hangs around his neck, fills his pipe, and tries several times to light it, but the breeze interferes. I stand up and move to his side to block the wind. The Wizard is focused on what he's doing and doesn't seem to notice. Eventually the fire takes, and he drags on his pipe. Then he turns and looks at me.

"What are you doing over there?"

"I blocked the wind." This doesn't register with him. "So you could light your pipe."

The Wizard looks from his pipe to me and back again, then rewards me with a broad grin. "Thank you!"

Finally he replies to my question, "I write on the blackboard whenever the voices in my head tell me to. This is a place for the insane to go. I have the credentials. I have the pedigree."

I wonder what the Wizard's life has been like, what kind of childhood he had, what kind of challenges he's faced. I thought of my own late brother, plagued for many years by schizophrenia—John would have loved it here in East Jesus. "We create a microcosm," the website says, "where those who fall through the cracks of the modern world may thrive."

"The crazies come here, the empaths," the Wizard continues. "Some who just plain want to get off the grid—they feel happier that way. There's some trauma in their past; they're running from something."

"Is there a drug problem in East Jesus?" I ask tentatively, because earlier the Wizard had mentioned his use of meth.

"The only drug problem we have are meth heads. We don't change. We get it under control. We survive. It takes one hell of a toll on the body, though. Yes and no, both. It is. Do good. Oh! Oh!" The Wizard interrupts himself again to tell me, excitedly, "We're hoarders! We never give anything away. Charlie Russell started the whole thing, named it East Jesus, made the T-shirt; he was a bit of a hermit. Charlie wanted to do a Burning Man 365, but you've got to pace yourself. It's not for amateurs."

The desert is not for amateurs—that's for sure.

"How many people live here?"

"Right now, off season, there are three of us here. We have solar panels, diesel backup, two refrigerators, a freezer and three air-conditioned rooms. It's too hot to support very many more people. Do you realize how much they drink? The bar bill! We're artists, gulp, gulp!" The Wizard mimes drinking a long, slow draft.

"What about short-term guests—do you get many of them?"

I'm imagining what it would be like to live in East Jesus—the heat, the isolation, the meth. Blinding sunshine, monotony, sand in your pants, a visitor, a donation ... bursts of creativity! More heat, more isolation, more meth....

"We've had three guests for a couple of days each in the last few months. It changes the balance. We have to exist here, so we have our own patterns. It's nice to have a change, but we're in this for the long run. We do it well. We don't talk too much to each other."

The art at East Jesus, more than 2,000 pieces, has all been donated over the past ten years. "Some pieces scream: *Look at me!*" the Wizard points out. "Others say: *You have to look for me to find me.* We have several acres of raw materials; we have a glass studio. A guy here named Pyro was really into glass. We have fuel and everything back there. We have a 110-volt welder; used it to repair the seesaw."

"Do you need any more materials?"

"No, but we need artists to come and work here. Ones who want to suffer for their art. We also accept money, alcohol—any really cool stuff."

"*You have to look for me to find me.*" The Wizard was talking about the art, but he might just as easily have been referring to other aspects of the desert: the East Jesus encampment itself, the freedom that comes with living off the grid, the beauty that grows from austerity—art from junk. He could have been talking about himself, a recovering addict who's been able to find joy in creativity, despite adversities.

I visited the desert again the following year, and drove over to East Jesus to say hello. My heart was light that morning; I was off to see the Wizard! The "En-Trance" sign was still there and so was the canopy, still casting a little square of shade over the Wizard's chair. But a thin young man (dressed all in black—in the desert) sat in the Wizard's place.

He was pale and friendly, and said the Wizard was no longer in East Jesus because he had gotten stuck in an ashram in India. He'd just flown over for a quick trip, but then got caught up in Covid-related flight cancellations and possibly other bureaucratic issues, and was unable to leave the country.

"You have to look for me to find me."

A view of the Grand Canyon, where the author and the Narcissist met, kissed and imagined the future.

Nankoweap for Me
Judy Zimola

"What would you do, Patsy? Heart-weary Queen of honkytonk jukeboxes and long nights with a longneck, what would you do if you were me?" Invoking The Cline's assistance isn't something I do at the flip of a beer cap. Patsy helps me with the heavy lifting, and right now I need her to tell it to me straight.

That morning began with mingling smells of coffee and juniper under the canopy of a flannel blue September sky. I lay on my back, gazing at the ochre cliffs as the Grand Canyon whispered tales of the dragonflies and short-horned lizards that inhabited the creek. Even cowgirls get the kinks though, so I tugged my T-shirt on while still under my sleeping bag, then stood and gave the canyon a back-popping, big-ass hug. Mark looked up from tending the coffee pot and, beaming, held aloft a blue speckled cup to entice me. *Oh hell,* I thought, *what have I done?*

Ten days had passed since our conservation group met for the first time in Kanab, Utah, where we got acquainted, organized supplies and caravanned to the North Rim. From there, we began our hike into the Little Nankoweap Canyon for five days of trail maintenance and four days of exploring.

The group's demographics ranged from Ned, an octogenarian who was rarely without his slide rule, to Nasir, a Pakistani daddy-o who channeled Miles Davis. Then there was Mark. Mark made an effort to talk to everybody. His swimmer's physique and classic blond good looks triggered my judginess. I pegged him as a narcissist. Probably did these working trips to show off his muscles.

After dinner on the second night, I took leave from the campfire to play with my planisphere. Once my butt found an agreeable contour in the smooth rocks, I brought the bottle of Jack Daniels out of my pack and poured a slug into my cup of water. Nightcap poured. Stars overhead. Contentment activated.

"Is this a private clambake or can anybody join?" an amiable voice asked from the dark.

Oh, great. The Narcissist wanted to show off. In light of the fact that we would be together for a while, I reasoned I should be polite. "I'm dusting off my stargazing skills. Sit down if you want."

Mark sat with his legs straight out on the stone, propping himself up with his elbows. "You have a planisphere," he observed.

Maybe he wasn't as dim as I thought. "Yes, but I'm having trouble seeing the print. Does that glow-in-the-dark stuff wear out, or is it me?"

"Did you expose it to light before you used it?" he politely asked.

Oh. "No. I forgot about that part." In pained silence I tried to gauge my level of jerkitude.

"You're from California, right?"

"Are you asking because you're curious or because I just now sounded like an airhead?"

The talk that followed came with lots of room around it, relaxed and feathery, in order not to disturb the stars' work.

"Do you have a boyfriend?" he asked.

"Shh. I'm identifying nebulae."

We didn't know each other well enough to parry further. But like the nightly round of the stars, that wheel would turn again.

Goofing off in the desert wilderness took some skill. Some members of the group were clearly uncomfortable being alone with their senses, filling the time with card games or talk of going to Vegas as soon as they got out of the canyon. Others wore the days like their bandanas, playing with shadows and light, searching out fossils, naming cliffs. Mark inhabited the canyon with grace, like the birds he noted in his journal.

"A male kestrel," he declared, sharing his binoculars with the octogenarian. "It looks young."

I forgave him for his good looks and grew to like him. He was smart in the ways of the outdoors. He knew the difference between crinoids and trilobites. A conversation could run from quoting *Charlotte's Web* to a description of the back streets of Turkey. He asked questions. And he could tell a good nighttime story.

I kept my distance.

The September days stretched out in a butter-colored silence, save for aspen leaves rustling and shimmering on the breeze. Free from the distractions of life above the rim, friendships deepened with each expanding day. One afternoon four of us hiked to a cliff to see what was on the other side. It took the better part of the morning to get there, and as soon as we arrived, we stretched out on the sun-warmed rocks and watched clouds, using daypacks for pillows.

Dozing, I was just about to dip into sleep when I felt a warm hand encircle my ankle. I turned my head enough to see that it was Mark. He didn't look at me for permission or confirmation, but kept up his conversation with Nasir about tenor sax players. I turned back to my cloud, wide-awake, really turned on.

The rest of the day was a tumble of horniness I tried in vain to ignore. A hawk catching a thermal etched a sensuous arc, and the stream's cool caress reminded me of Mark's touch. Mischievous breezes whispered secrets about hidden coves with beds of soft pine needles. Even the trail mix seduced.

The campfire that night carved a little room out of the darkness. The warm air rose up and up as the canyon floor cooled, its walls silhouetted against that knowing, winking sky. Mark sat with his back against a rock and beckoned me by patting the ground in front of him. It was exactly what I didn't need and exactly what I hankered for. I scooted in and snuggled against his chest. His arms circled my waist; the ebb and flow of his breathing felt nice against my back. He kissed the top of my head, then took a big breath. I braced for what was coming.

"What about your boyfriend?"

Right. What about William. William had a cool job with the state and a nice car and a funny cat, but the best part was the 100 miles between us. His recent hints of seriousness were flattering, but the idea of living with him in a ranch house in suburban Sacramento made my neck itch. The recent boundless days had opened me to the discovery that I was good on my own, without romantic ties. To anyone.

"It's not going to work out," I said simply. I didn't say, "It's not going to work out with anybody right now." Because despite Mark's grace and intelligence, the "us" that was taking shape existed only in the cradle of the canyon's red stone cliffs. I wanted to stay a wild thing, always part of Nankoweap's ancient rhythm.

I didn't bother to share these epiphanies. Instead, I kissed him.

From that moment until we got into our respective cars two days later, Mark and I were intertwined. I tried to let the hours go lightly but Mark gave them gravity, and between thirsty kisses he planned our six-month reunion. I played along the entire way, right up to when we said our good-byes in the parking lot.

Nasir's jaunty salute coaxed a laugh as I watched the last of the group depart, save for Mark. He was fussing with something in the trunk of his car, and as he crossed the gravel toward me, it was obvious he was hiding something behind his back. Tears came quickly and stung. I cried at leaving Nankoweap's generosity of spirit and unassuming gifts, but her big heart also exposed my selfishness, and for that I couldn't look Mark in the eye.

He took me in his arms and, voice quavering, explained the gift. "I took your empty whiskey bottle when you weren't looking." He pulled back just enough to hand it to me, pressing my hands with his around the cool glass. "I filled it with water from the creek. Don't read what I wrote on it until you get where you're going tonight, OK?"

"No, I won't." I choked.

"Jackson Hole in February. Dress warm!"

"Ha ha, you bet!"

"OK then, drive safe. I'll be in touch." A quick kiss and then off we went, down that lonesome, scrubby, sunbaked highway, him to Flagstaff and me back to Kanab for a night. I pop Patsy into the CD player, and she croons of weeping willows and falling to pieces and faded love for the whole hour-and-a-half drive.

The only thing I'm comfortable with my first night back in civilization is the warm shower. Everything else is too much: the motel room too taupe, the air too conditioned, the light too incandescent. Or maybe I'm just not ready to come back and deal.

The motel rooms surround a little lawn area, where I take my backpack with its heavy gift.

Ten days ago I started this trip here in Kanab. I didn't know Mark, or Nasir or the octogenarian, or how the canyon bends and folds time, layering still, sunny days with red dirt, campfire stories, pine's whispers, and soft kisses. Removing the bottle from its nest of T-shirts and socks at the bottom of the pack feels like I'm reliving a memory that hasn't even happened yet. On it, in black indelible pen, Mark inscribed, "If you can imagine it, you can begin it."

I'm an ass. Even Patsy agrees.

Desert artist Noah Purifoy created fantastical sculptures from found objects.

OLD BOOTS, NEW VISION
Peg Wendling Gerdes

Drifts and rumors of Noah Purifoy's Outdoor Desert Art Museum of Assemblage Sculpture had first reached me in San Francisco in the early 1990s, when my husband had a store on Haight Street that sponsored local artists. It was then, too, that our enjoyment of—no, reverence for—found objects emerged. We were, at that time, working with artists who took little bits of nothing and turned those bits into beautiful and often provocative creations that filled people with wonder and delight. Purifoy's installations had already turned into a mythical place arising in the desert by the time we first visited.

Noah Purifoy created a timeless wonderment out of thin air up near Joshua Tree, California. We had driven up into the hills near Joshua Tree from Palm Springs, where the winding road, elevation and change of terrain all signaled a distinct transformation in scenery and environment. Windswept, mostly uninhabited, filled with high desert sand and random vegetation, there is a spacious silence. Here, Joshua trees, those famous spiky yucca-like plants, flaunt adaptability in the desert and stark beauty to the ecological world.

As we parked the car across from the Outdoor Desert Art Museum we realized this was no mundane tourist attraction with tickets or maps or attendants. This seemed unusual even for a remote stretch of desert, under wide skies, freckled with what at first looked like … junk. *What? Was this really a museum?* The lack of ceremony made us pay attention in a different way. As far as we could see, arranged with an unexplained order, stood constructions of all shapes and sizes, made of wood, cast-off metal, bicycle tires, appliances, old computer monitors, stone, flowerpots, brass headboards, and fabric rotting in the sun and wind. It looked like a cross between an old movie set and a car parts junkyard. We were the only visitors, which we later realized is not at all uncommon.

My boots were covered with fine, tawny dust before I even made it past the ramshackle gate, a hodge-podge of rusted metal planes and poles. A chain-link barrier adorned with padlocks, forlorn and useless, hung between two posts, with no accompanying fence. The thought struck me: Maybe it wasn't forlorn at all, maybe it was jaunty and intentional. In fact, this unlocked fence, like much of Purifoy's work, suggests irony.

Even Noah Purifoy's name evokes a kind of wonder, a bit of poetry. Say it out loud: *Purifoy.* An African-American, born in Alabama in 1917, Purifoy served in WWII's naval force and then made his way to California, part of the Great Migration from the violent and racially segregated South. He was the first full-time Black student to earn his BFA at CalArts, then called Chouinard Art Institute, in 1956.

Purifoy become renowned for his art in Los Angeles, especially for his repurposing of broken and damaged goods from the 1964 Watts Riots, an endeavor in itself deeply generous and creative. In

Old Boots, New Vision — Peg Wendling Gerdes

1989, he moved to the high desert near Joshua Tree to turn a friend's ten scrubby desert acres into a neighborhood of arrangements that tell stories of home, hope, social justice and everyday life. He applied the same creative sensibilities that won him deep respect and followers in LA. In doing so, he thumbed his nose at urban strictures on *what art is*, constructing with found objects, so-called "junk" that is no longer useful in its original form. Newly recombined in ways playful and searing, profound and surprising, the forms are now strikingly useful once more.

Truly a neighborhood of castoff materials, the museum reminds visitors of original families, ways of life, communities, social structures and methods long gone. We went down one route, and the neighborhood was casually poignant and mysterious, sometimes hard-hitting with an in-your-face attitude. Taking another turn, we found it fond and laugh-out-loud funny. It invites interaction and exploration—we inspected a little room, climbed a set of stairs, pondered legs in workpants with shoes planted on a high ridge ... and was that the Golden Gate Bridge over there?

I've been reminded several times of a mandala when visiting: a spiritual place that is organized according to a deeper life rhythm, changed constantly by the elements. A rhythm, not perhaps as fast as sand that disperses with the tide or wafts away in the breeze, an inevitable and continual rearrangement: rusting, rotting items blowing in the wind. It is altered a bit or a lot every time you see it, by the elements that have taken over tending of Purifoy's work. It's now a legacy that weathers, withers and rusts at its own pace.

What is our relationship to found objects and junk in a culture where "new" is king? Discarded and maybe no longer useful for its original purpose, junk may still be functional in a new way, especially when juxtaposed with other elements. There is order in the seeming disorder. These discarded objects were carefully and playfully arranged, disassembled, then re-assembled—and now nature is rearranging them again.

Each time I've visited, my favorite object has changed, as the Purifoy neighborhoods have changed. These days, clear walkways have been added, and there's lots of signage explaining Purifoy's art.

But the creatively chaotic spirit of the place remains the same. On one special visit, I knelt down in front of a whimsical pair of old boots with poles stuck in them—legs, for sure—and a big block of stuck-together wooden sticks hovering above, suggesting a body about to step forward. It hit me then: This wreckage is a sign of life—long-worn and perhaps long-loved boots that had hiked many miles—still offering up stamina and vigor to the viewer. The boots are still on their way somewhere, humming with energy and marching into the future, scuffed up, lively and full of spirit. Maybe that's what Purifoy was after, all along.

Visitors wait for a sound bath outside the Integratron.

BLISSED OUT AT THE INTEGRATRON:
WHERE ART, SCIENCE AND MAGIC CONVERGE

Laurie McAndish King

"If you want to find the secrets of the universe," Nikola Tesla once said, "think in terms of energy, frequency and vibration." Tesla probably knew what he was talking about; he was the innovative genius who brought us alternating current and countless other electrical inventions. But I wasn't sure how to take advantage of this wisdom until a friend told me the vibrational "sound baths" at a place called the Integratron can be life-changing. I had a long weekend coming up—and of course I want to learn the secrets of the universe—so I planned a road trip.

To visit the Integratron you must first travel through miles of Mojave Desert to the tiny, earthquake-prone community of Landers, California. It's a desolate area, and, depending on the direction of your approach, you may come across long, straight roads with names like *Mars, Saturn* and *Moon*, and warnings that those roads are not maintained. You may notice signs alerting drivers to dangerously high winds, or the hand-painted one proclaiming "Truth Wins—This is the Day!" Occasionally you'll see huge clusters of mailboxes—twenty or thirty or more—huddled together by the side of the road, with no actual houses in sight.

You're not likely to miss the lonely looking "Wine and Rock" shop with a three-foot statue of a space alien near the front door. It's the common gray kind of alien with a large head. You will pass scrawny Joshua trees and dry bunchgrass and tumbleweed that collects into vaguely menacing sculptures strewn across the desert. The white spines of cholla cactus will glow in the sunlight.

About twenty miles north of Yucca Valley you will finally see a bright white dome, thirty-eight feet high and fifty-five feet in diameter, jutting out of the honey-colored desert. This is the Integratron, the one-of-a-kind acoustical palace where I am headed for my first sound bath. I'll get to experience a fusion of art, science and magic, according to the website. It says the full-body vibrational experience is deeply relaxing and rejuvenating. And that, for those who are open to it, sound lets us move beyond the human realm into the "all are field" experience, where we can access a greater part of self, or of other beings. Apparently, it can even be psychedelic.

My real curiosity lies with the Integratron dome itself—the structure within which the sound bath will take place. Begun in the late 1950s by aviation engineer George Van Tassel, the Integratron was designed to deliver healing "cellular rejuvenation therapy" to humans. The engineering marvel was said to be inspired by the Great Pyramid, Moses' Tabernacle, and the writings of Nicola Tesla. The actual plans were given to Van Tassel both verbally and telepathically by an extraterrestrial named Solganda while they were both aboard a spacecraft piloted by beings from the planet Venus. Or so he said.

Van Tassel explained that these beings were providing the formula for rejuvenating tissue because, in their judgment, humans were making such a mess of things on Earth. With our limited lifespans, we simply didn't have enough time to develop the moral and spiritual maturity necessary to sustain civilization. However, by exposing ourselves to the Integratron's high-voltage electrostatic generation, humans could easily extend their lifetimes by twenty to fifty years, or even more. We would be happier, healthier and wiser. The Integratron would also help Earthlings develop anti-gravity and time-travel capabilities.

As you might imagine, the Integratron is the only instrument of its kind on the planet. And it's on National Register of Historic Places. Who wouldn't want to visit?

As I pulled into the Integratron parking lot, long clouds hovered in a brilliant blue sky. A green patch of eucalyptus and small fruit trees surrounded the bone-white Integratron, which arched across the horizon like an observatory. A Harley with two UFO stickers sat in a swirl of dust.

Van Tassel chose this site carefully. It is just a few miles from a monument known as Giant Rock, where he had been leading weekly meditation sessions with hundreds of other UFO enthusiasts. Giant Rock, possibly the world's largest free-standing boulder, is a sacred area for Native Americans. It has its own eccentric history involving underground chambers, the FBI, and unusually strong piezoelectric activity. Van Tassel hosted many annual UFO conferences there; the largest was said to be attended by 11,000 believers. He also opened and ran the Giant Rock Interplanetary Airport, as well as the airport café.

But this particular location, the one he chose for the Integratron, marks the convergence of nine ley lines and three underground rivers, making it the site of an extraordinary geomagnetic vortex. Not to mention that it's out in the high desert in a place that, at the time it was constructed, would have been remote. The harsh climate, arid landscape and rattlesnakes no doubt helped keep curiosity-seekers away.

But they're here today, in full force, because the Integratron now sits in the center of an oasis. An oasis with shaded hammocks and cool lemon-water and a gift shop offering crystals and glow-in-the-dark T-shirts and CDs of sound-bath meditations (Compassion, Gratitude, Healing) recorded by the various sound therapists who work here.

A friendly man called Boo Lane works in the gift shop. Boo is tall, thin, bald, and wears a white goatee and round John Lennon-style glasses. His T-shirt has an image of the California Republic Bear Flag. He is also training to be a ranger at Burning Man. Boo says the Integratron doesn't do any advertising, except for supporting music festivals. They're always busy, though, because Huell Howser put them on the map when he featured the Integratron in his "California Gold" TV show for PBS.

I bought an Integratron refrigerator magnet and a crystal for a friend with an upcoming surgery, and Boo said the crystal had been charged right there at the vortex, so it would be powerful.

When it was time to begin our sound bath, a tall young woman came by to check that everyone had their tickets. Her hair was in dreads, and big flowy letters on her T-shirt read *Sex, Kush & Hip Hop*. Because we were all scattered about in the hammocks, Ms. Sex, Kush & Hip Hop had to shout to be heard: "OK, everyone!" she hollered, waving her arm. "Let's go bliss out!"

Inside the circular first floor, it's all blond wood, laminated and varnished, very ship-shape. A low-ceilinged museum presents the history of George Van Tassel and the Integratron. The aviator, inventor and transmitter of extraterrestrial intelligence was born in 1910 in Ohio and moved to California when he was twenty. He worked at Edwards Air Force Base and for Lockheed, Douglas Aircraft and Hughes Aviation, where he inspected aircraft for Howard Hughes. Mr. Hughes was said to have flown to the Giant Rock Airport café on weekends so he could eat a piece of Mrs. Van Tassel's pie.

In addition to Van Tassel's extensive electrical knowledge, his considerable personal charm and sensitivity to spiritual matters made him an excellent candidate for receiving alien blueprints. Those Giant Rock meditation sessions led, in 1953, to the first of his many contacts with extraterrestrials.

This is where he got the information about how to rejuvenate living cells. The Integratron's huge, non-ferromagnetic wooden dome with a rotating metal electrostatic dirod on the outside would effectively generate its own lightning, which would be pulled into the building, creating the rejuvenating effect. A fifty-thousand-volt capacitor was somehow involved. Up to ten thousand people a day could simply walk through the activated Integratron and experience life-extending cellular rejuvenation. It would be a marvelous gift to humanity.

A charismatic speaker, Van Tassel was a guest lecturer at many colleges and universities, and appeared on more than 400 radio and television shows. By 1957 he had raised enough money to begin building the Integratron. Howard Hughes was one of many enthusiastic funders.

There were apparently setbacks along the way, however, so the Integratron had to be built in fits and starts. It was nearly complete twenty years later, in 1978, when George Van Tassel died of an apparent heart attack while preparing for a TV interview. Members of his family were suspicious, as the 68-year-old Van Tassel was healthy and had suffered no warning signs of an attack. Some people believe he was getting too close to proving groundbreaking science, and had to be silenced.

There was also the matter of Van Tassel's second wife, the only person with him at the time he died. Her two previous husbands are also rumored to have died under suspect circumstances. And I didn't get the details on how this happened, but apparently a space entity named Lo channeled Van Tassel's epitaph: "Birth through Induction, Death through Short Circuit."

Within days of his death, all Van Tassel's Integratron research, journals, drawings and notes had been stolen or mysteriously disappeared—or they were in the outbuildings bulldozed by the Bureau of Land Management, depending on your sources. Thus the Integratron's promise to rejuvenate the human body has, unfortunately, gone untested. There wasn't time to see everything in the museum before our sound bath, but I got the general idea.

Slowly, one by one, our group filed to the back of the room and climbed the steep, ladder-like steps to the second floor of the structure Van Tassel referred to as a tabernacle. I was swept back to my childhood, and the song "We are Climbing Jacob's Ladder" edged its way into my mind: Jacob's Ladder, the Stairway to Heaven, the link between humans and the divine in Christian, Jewish, and Islamic traditions. The Ladder of Enlightenment in Hinduism. Ladders, a symbol of spiritual journey in many Native American religions. Van Tassel's alien friends definitely got that part right.

We climbed through a square hole in the ceiling/floor into the upper chamber of the Integratron. At eye level, a series of small windows provides natural light between the sixteen huge, beamed ribs reaching to the ceiling high above. The inside is made completely of wood, giving visitors the impression they're inside a gigantic ship's hull or, as the Integratron's literature more poetically suggests, a huge cello. Either way, it's said to be acoustically perfect. And it's gorgeous.

Beneath one of the windows a small table serves as an altar, which is filled with crystals, feathers, engraved stones, Mother Mary statuettes, a framed photo of Paramahansa Yogananda and other devotional objects. An automobile license plate proclaims "♥ YO NBR." Love your neighbor.

Circled around the center of the room were thirty-five identical mats, each with a pillow. Two dozen or so crystal bowls, straight-sided, translucent white, in multiple sizes, sat in their own little circle toward one edge of the room. The largest was about twenty inches in diameter. These were the bowls that would soon resonate with relaxing, rejuvenating euphonics. Even if it didn't deliver the secrets of the universe or the cellular-level rejuvenation promised by the Integratron, this sound bath might be the next best thing.

I chose a mat, lay down, and gazed up at the huge wooden dome overhead. Dreyton, our musical therapist-guide, told us he'd been playing bowls for more than eighteen years. "We have thirty-five people in this space four times a day. Five times on Fridays and Saturdays. You have to make reservations months in advance. We tried fitting fifty people in at once, but it was just too crowded."

"The sound is pervasive," he continued, "but not invasive. It will get up to ninety decibels, but don't worry—it won't hurt your ears. Just relax and get into the experience."

As we relaxed, Dreyton explained about the rubber-tipped wooden rods he used to play the bowls, the non-denominational angels who often visited, and the nine ley lines—which "are like acupuncture meridians, but for the earth."
I guess he knew his audience.
He went on for a while, but all I remember is that the "sound-coherentizing geometry of the parabolic dome"—or maybe it was the "vortexian mechanics of the entire building"—creates a coherent field, which is why the sound is able to generate its direct cellular effect.
"This music is always unique," Dreyton continued. "It can be played loudly or softly, more or less melodically, with a different emphasis each time." He would focus on three notes today: C for the first chakra, F for the heart and B for the crown.
Dreyton had explained that people are often so relaxed during the sound bath that they drift off to sleep. If the person next to you begins to snore, he directed, just give a polite little nudge to wake them up.
I closed my eyes.
At first there was only silence.
Then breath.
Next, slowly, the faintest of hums, just one low, sonorous tone, barely audible.
Eventually a second tone began, and then a third. They blended together, separated and blended again. *Not really much happening here,* I thought. It *was* relaxing, though.
I took a moment to consider the Integratron's provenance. *Was the design really inspired by the Great Pyramid? If so, why was the Integratron dome-shaped? Same issue with Moses' Tabernacle. The part about Tesla made a little more sense because of the electrical*

aspect: A Tesla coil is an electrical resonant transformer circuit used to produce high-voltage, low-current, high-frequency alternating-current electricity. I looked it up before I came, but I still don't understand what it does.

My fingertips began to tingle. The vibrations grew more intense, louder and louder until I felt a hum in my throat. Church bells. The tones began to waver, then warble, waa-waa-waaaaa-waa, varying in length and intensity. Once I *felt* the waves overlap near my heart—that would have been the constructive coherence of the waves, when two intersect and combine to create a wave of greater amplitude. That part was genuinely trippy!

And, in retrospect, maybe a little scary, because *if I could actually feel these sound waves in my body, could they disrupt my brain waves, or my heartbeat, or some other vital function? Why had I allowed myself to go forward with this experience without researching it thoroughly? Was this the way the aliens would finally control Earthlings?*

The old me might have indulged these worries—and more. But the rejuvenated me didn't care. Even without knowing the secrets of the universe, I was blissed out.

Many Indigenous cultures use a figure that's a combination of human and animal to represent the shaman's connection with the spirit world.

The Shaman's Cave
MJ Pramik

Many deserts have a shaman's cave. Or, at least, the rumor of one. The speculation that one exists brings with it a sense of anticipation. The wilderness expanse of sand, rocks, cacti, pokeweed and chaparral at the base of the San Jacinto Mountains in Southern California's Palm Desert is no exception.

In the gray December of 2022, ending the third year of Covid, I made a pilgrimage to a friend's desert hideaway that served as a retreat away from the usual family hullabaloo. We lingered over the holiday tradition of butter cookie baking, hot chocolate, board games, Yahtzee and tinkling Frank Sinatra songs in the background. A dark night howled outside the small house huddled against the chill as winter winds slid down the San Jacinto Mountains into the valley.

My friend and her local guests discussed the ancient desert lore about Snow Creek, an enclave of thirty-seven dwellings around twelve miles from Palm Springs. They whispered about a "shaman's cave" as we celebrated New Year's Eve in Snow Creek.

"A shaman's cave?" My voice revealed my excitement. I'm always up for a magical spiritual adventure. "I'll get up early and pack the food. How far is it from here?"

"A short distance up to the base of Mt. Jacinto," said Maddy.

"Then a few more miles," said Alex, her boyfriend.

"How many miles is a few?" I pushed for a more definitive answer.

"You won't need your hiking poles," said Bobby.

Maddy's seven-year-old niece Char grumbled about being "too tired." Her nine-year-old brother Hen stood up and touched his toes. "I'll be ready to climb that mountain," he said. "Come on, Char, five to ten miles is not far. And it's downhill on the way home."

"Do you know the location of this fabled grotto?" I asked.

"No, we don't," said Maddy. They had lived in the area for about two years, but as yet had not visited the shaman's cave.

"So how do we find this shaman house?" I asked as we tidied up the dishes. The adults all nodded at the dark window, out there toward the mountain. We set our plans for early morning, eight o'clock in the chilled air, ready for hard-frozen soil and the wind blustering invisible over the uneven ankle-turning surface.

The call of wilderness pulled us like a compass needle at the thin crack of dawn. Soaring mountains lured us toward the snow-capped peaks to the south. A hawk's circling flight beckoned us to follow it up the cragged boulders. San Jacinto Peak loomed above us at 10,834 feet. Fog smoke puffed from all our mouths. It...was...cold.

Beneath the buzz of this world roars a hum of the underworld, the song of those who once walked over the same rocks we stepped upon. The desert on which we trod had housed many thousands of human and nonhuman animals, all of which had crunched the pebbles and bones of those that came before us. I believe we all have a need within us to feel past spirits as we step on the desert floor. Whenever I visit the Mojave, these spirits seem to walk with me and my friends, as they did in our quest for the rumored shaman's cave.

On a paper map, this stretch of the Coachella Valley sweeps along the eastern border of the San Jacinto range. Touching several towns and cities with famous names—Palm Springs, Palm Desert, Coachella, Indio, Rancho Mirage—it borders the Salton Sea and trespasses Mount San Gorgonio to the north.

But we didn't have a paper map this January 1. Char and Hen charged out toward the mountain. I'd wrapped our sustenance tight and asked the stronger hikers to carry the bundles.

I did bring my collapsible hiking poles. And learned this was not a good idea. Tumbleweeds and low-lying vegetation snarled my progress. Collapsed, the poles fit into someone's backpack.

"Whose cave is this?" I asked.

"We don't know. Someday we'll check out the Agua Caliente Cultural Museum in Palm Springs. They're supposed to have archives, a library, even a film festival," Maddy said against the wind.

We had hiked up a slight rocky incline from the house where we holidayed. Ponderosa pine, white fir, incense cedar and manzanita pocked the altitude above us. As we trudged through rock-strewn grasslands and chapparal, brittle spikes of witch grass, horsetail and other plants caught at our pants legs, causing several stumbles over the desert floor. Bushes and sagebrush reached up at our legs and slowed our pace. It was as if the desert did not want us to discover the shaman's hideout.

After an hour's climb, we spied what looked like a structure, although it was not exactly a cave. Two ravens convened high on the rocky peak of an edifice constructed of several granite slabs randomly leaning against each other. It looked as if an earthquake from long ago had adjusted the "walls" of the structure. Recent humans (I suspected county safety staff) had closed off the three openings with red reinforced steel bars to protect hikers like our band from squeezing into the haphazard space.

I stepped lightly around the slabs of stone leaning against each other. The shallow structure stood strewn with desert debris. The towering emptiness of the cave supported my hope that the desert can return a person to her true self. Cold, rough-hewn wedges and hunks of granite testified that surviving in a desert cave would grow a person's inner strength. I leaned against the outer wall and considered a night spent here—it would certainly toughen my spirit.

As our group began the descent home in the rapidly freezing winds, I squinted into the shaman's cave one last time, squeezing the frigid rebar. My gaze wandered over the desert that had once served the legendary shaman and his Agua Caliente Band of Cahuilla Indians. Dusk enveloped us as we became shadows to each other. Out of the darkening cave an enormous bird swooped over our heads. I felt the wind from its outspread wings sweep past my cheeks.

I stood on the barren, rocky ground, my hiking boots clinging to the planet's surface. Turning southward toward the opening of the shaman's cave, I saw shapes in the dusk and felt the spirit beings whirling in the coming darkness.

I would later learn that for centuries the Cahuilla people have inhabited the desert where we stood. Many of the Agua Caliente Band of Cahuilla Indians now live on the Agua Caliente Indian Reservation near Palm Springs. After returning from the hike to the shaman's cave, I read *Temalpakh* and *Mukat's People*, the authoritative books by scholar Dr. Lowell John Bean about this tribe.

In *Mukat's People*, Dr. Bean recounts that the Cahuilla honor Mukat as their creator god. According to their creation story, creator god Mukat and another spirit god Temayuwat, birthed from the union of twin balls of lightning, *Amnaa* (Power) and *Tukmiut* (Night). Mukat reigns as the basic energy source from which all things were created.

In one legend in *Mukat's People*, I learned about a cannibal living in a glass cave near Tahquitz Peak on Mt. San Jacinto. This creature—both animal and human—spent its days eavesdropping and snooping on the inhabitants of the desert near the current Palm Springs. The spirit would return at night to eat them alive and would hold their souls for eternity. Another tale claimed the creator spirit Mukat slowly became corrupted like many desert inhabitants around the San Jacinto peaks. Mukat turned from being a moral creator to using his mighty powers to harm others.

Dr. Bean's latest book is *Time Immemorial: The Traditional Ways and History of the Members of the Agua Caliente Indian Reservation*, published in 2020. In this volume, Dr. Bean writes, "For the Cahuilla, the religious and political leaders and shamans within any particular group are highly creative people who enter into 'dream states' from which new ideas emerged and would then be incorporated into the culture of that person's group…"

Those Cahuilla shamanic *puvalams*, or priests, had many roles. They practiced desert medicine and underwent ritual training and initiation. A member of a secret society within the tribe, a puvalam had to possess supernatural power and be called to the life of a shaman. He had to risk misfortune or death. He had to create and own his specific songs and dances. He had to show his true spirit guardian. He had to be up to tasks like predicting rain, forecasting big weather events, or warning of seismic shifts in the mountains and desert. He knew how to cure snake bite and predict a falling star. His group within the tribe often acted together and influenced the political structure of the settlement. He had to innovate, create, and cope with unexpected events. The Cahuilla shaman was a diviner, a dreamer.

I remember peering into that cave. In retrospect, I wonder if I were sensing that one of Mukat's shamans might be looking out at me. With my active imagination, I could feel that this high priest still guarded the rocks and cave.

As the wind whistled over the land, I imagined I heard the echo of the shaman's songs. Perhaps the rattlesnake and bobcat hiding among the crevices and overhangs also felt the power of his dances.

I looked up. A meteor streaked across the sky.

An owl screeched in the distance.

Zabriskie Point painting by Gerald Brommer

BROMMER'S PALETTE
Linda Watanabe McFerrin

—after a conversation with Gerald Brommer,
Death Valley, December

Month One

I still don't understand Zabriskie Point—
rose pink, cinder, agate . . .
I've had to find a whole new palette this far from seashore,
terrain I understand—
periwinkle, conch . . .
I think it's been a month.
I've been searching for a month—
sea bottom, coral (fan and branch).

Anchor it with *blue*.

I'm painting-in flora where it isn't—
desert holly, sage, a plant called Mormon's Tea . . .
It's hard to fathom living rock—

leopardskin, feldspar, onyx . . .
but yesterday; it started to speak me,
my hand against the corrugated crumble of dry mud,
so warm: a giant generator, there, beneath the earth.

It's beginning to come clear.

Month Two

The desert eats time, distance.
The tracks of kangaroo rats and kit foxes in the dunes beguile me.

I've lost another day.

Month Three

I thought I'd found the palette I was seeking,
thought I'd begun to work with it—
sulphur, madder, manganese . . .
The colors have been working me.
I think I am as yellow as the hills.

Time's gotten away from me.

Month Four

She came up through the badlands under Manly Peak,
a solitary hiker.

She seemed like a mirage.
I should have stopped her, asked her to coffee—
something.

Everything slips through my hands.

Month Five

Yesterday some tourists found their way out here.
Their talk was strange to me—
they could have been ravens calling, asses braying, coyotes.
They asked a lot of questions, tried to buy a painting.

I like the desert best when it is silent.

If everything is quiet,
I can hear it hum.

Month Six

———

Redemption

"A lone coyote howled in the distance."

Peak Experiences on a Desert Plain
Daphne Beyers

The flat sands of the Anza-Borrego Desert stretched for miles around me. In the far distance, a mountain peak burned like a torch as it caught the last light of the setting sun. Then the torch winked out, and a cool breeze stirred the tiny brittlebush shrubs spotting the sand. A hummingbird buzzed, its wings a blur. It settled on a taller shrub, then darted off. My only companion, gone.

As the sky darkened, the sands turned to hues of lavender and purple. Night changes the desert more than other landscapes. When the sun's relentless, burning eye closes, another eye opens, one rarely felt in cities and forests. This is the eye of feeling, of seeing the unseen. I had come to the desert at a turning point in my life, a time when I felt, as the poet Wordsworth once said, that the world was too much with me. Too loud, too crazy, too much, and yet so empty of meaning and purpose. A great phantasmal circus of color and sound, signifying nothing. My heart craved something more, something really real, and there is nothing more real on earth than the desert. Stripped of houses and cars and shopping malls, stripped of all the hoopla of daily comings and goings, the desert sits in stillness.

I settled down on the sand, using my tattered sleeping bag as a cushion. I had water and a sandwich for later. My car was a couple miles away, parked on the side of the desert highway. I felt alone and vulnerable, but I was not afraid. There are predators in the desert, but far fewer than the human predators you find at night in cities and country towns.

The colors drained from my surroundings as dusk settled into night. A lone coyote howled in the distance. A moment later, another coyote called in response. Then another. Then a whole chorus of howls rose in a crescendo. There must have been twenty of them. Their howls rose higher in pitch. Then, in the midst of that chorus, another screech emerged. A high-pitched, unearthly cackle, unlike anything I had ever heard before, screamed, cracking the night a full octave above the din. The screech rose higher and higher into a shriek. It seemed almost human, but no human could make such a sound at such a distance. In the desert at night, it may not have even been a living thing.

Then the shriek and the howls cut off as if an unseen maestro's hand had silenced them. I wondered if I should leave. I was no match for a pack of coyotes, especially one led by some inhuman witch creature. I felt no fear, but how could I trust my own city-honed instincts in a strange land ruled by nature's incomprehensible laws? I had traveled too far to give up my quest for meaning so soon, but I had to be safe and not stupid. I looked around for a sign. Should I stay or should I go?

A shadow darted a few yards from my seat. Had the coyotes found me? The shadow hopped. I looked closer, and the shadow resolved into a gentle bunny rabbit. The bunny appeared totally unconcerned with the chorus of howls that had just ended. If that bunny wasn't worried, the coyotes must be further away than they sounded. I took it as a sign and decided to stay. It was a big desert after all. Miles and miles of desert. The coyotes' noses were attuned to their natural prey. Sure, they'd opportunistically eat me if they came across me, but they weren't actually hunting for humans.

True night came to the desert. The moon hadn't risen yet, and a deepening darkness covered the sands. Above, millions and millions of stars appeared, twinkling clusters of pinprick whites, so many that they obscured the familiar constellations I could see from home, the ones bright enough to shine through the miasma of city lights.

So many stars! And around each one a possible world like ours full of mystery and wonder. All these worlds shining in the night sky, their light undimmed by distance and time. This is what I was searching for. Not just an escape from the apocalyptic noise of a world on fire with upheaval and change, but a way to touch the still point of eternity, if only for a moment. One perfect moment when the world stops, thoughts stop, the mind of worry and confusion falls away, and what remains is the real, unchanging reality of existence. I sat under the light of distant stars and felt a deep sense of peace. I felt grounded, my spine a tree with roots passing through layers of sand and stone down to the deepest heart of the world, its branches spreading far above the earth, through space and time with stars as leaves.

People search for miracles, miracles of healing or riches or finding someone to love, when all along we are surrounded by the real miracle of existence, of simply being alive in a world of indescribable beauty and joy. We are like fish searching for water while swimming through an endless ocean. We forget what matters most in life. We forget to love.

I ate my sandwich and packed up my things. I hadn't planned

to sleep alone in the desert. That is never a good idea, and certainly not with a pack of coyotes wandering the area. The moon rose, its gentle light shining across the sand as I made my way back to my car. I remembered the time I had slept overnight in the Mojave Desert with a group of friends. There was safety in numbers, and one friend was armed in case of trouble.

That night I'd slept a deep, dreamless sleep on the hard-packed sand until a noise woke me. I'd heard what sounded like the clear, high note of a trumpet followed by a choir of angelic voices rising to a deafening peak. The thunderous roar jerked me awake. I sat up to absolute silence. My friends were sound asleep. No one was playing a trumpet or singing. There was no sound at all except the quiet whisper of a breeze. The sky paled from black to navy to lighter blue at the horizon. There, heralded by blushing hues of pink and red, rose the golden orb of the sun. In my sleep, my inner ear had heard the choir of morning, the voice of the desert singing its love to the dawn light of the returning sun.

This is the miracle of existence. There may be no such thing as time, as Einstein proposes. But there is day and night, light and dark, yin and yang, forever spinning and revolving one into the other, ever changing and yet eternally the same. Somewhere in the center of all that spinning is the still point, the fulcrum of eternity, perhaps the finger of God. That center is also our center, the very center of our hearts where we touch reality, and where reality touches us. When the heart drinks this water, the parched desert plains inside us fill to the brim and overflow with the waters of love and joy, peace and understanding. The world doesn't change. We do. And that makes all the difference.

On the road from Sedona to Flagstaff

From Sedona to Flagstaff and Back: The Road to Redemption
Joanna Biggar

There are some places where you can never be a tourist. These are places already visited that have left such an imprint on you, the traveler, that any subsequent visits can only be experienced by the haunting of the first. For me, Flagstaff and Sedona, towns in northern Arizona, and the road that connects them through wondrous Oak Creek Canyon are such places.

My second visit to the area was for a completely celebratory occasion: a joyous fiftieth wedding reunion. But although I saw its highlights, its vistas and town squares, its galleries, shops and historic buildings, breathed its famed clear, high-elevation air and enjoyed its renewed prosperity, I could only acknowledge them through the lens of my first trip, two years before. It was then that I traced the same route in search of a child, a young teen wounded in body and in spirit, beloved by her family, but—although she was physically with me—lost to us. And we wanted to call her home.

Tatum had been suffering for two years from a variety of afflictions that can capture young people who have devastating encounters that are reinforced by a toxic social environment and bad choices. Her case was also amplified by social media and the isolation brought on by the Pandemic. And with so many of our youth undergoing similar situations, in the worst sense, she was not alone. However, she felt very alone, and among other things, she was depressed. After several other approaches to helping her, she was enrolled in a therapeutic boarding school program outside Sedona. Along with her parents and siblings, my husband and I took part in a planned family visit. We fervently wished the beauty of the area would play a large role in healing Tatum, for she was a girl susceptible to the power of beauty and nature. And in my own case, I, too, clung to the power of that landscape to give me hope.

The second visit, the celebratory one, as I said, brought me to many of the same places I had been to the first time. In a way, the two towns—Flagstaff mountain, Sedona desert—visibly very different from each other, are still quintessentially American towns of the West. Flagstaff with its old-timey buildings and historic square, open vistas, astronomy center, and pink brick Catholic Church of the Nativity of the Blessed Virgin, shouts out its Old West credentials. It once boasted having more bars than all other establishments combined, eventually became a prosperous railway hub, and then settled into its enduring image as a major stop on Route 66.

Sedona, on the other hand, with its other-worldly red rock formations and barren, dramatic landscapes, became a favorite spot for shooting early westerns, with Zane Gray writing a novel about it, John Wayne and even Elvis making movies there. But in the

1950s a woman named Mary Lou Keller found other riches in its topography and declared it a global center of spiritual energy. Tarot cards, crystals, palm readings, practices taken from Native Americans, and the supposed "vortexes of energy" then followed —and remain today. Spiritual seekers of all stripes converge there in large numbers, a phenomenon which also marks the town as peculiarly American.

On the second trip, although I was able to see the surface of these tourist attractions, my vision was still focused on my earlier visit with Tatum. Our whole family had spent time together for meals at a lovely lodge, but Tatum, capable of her huge smiles, was mostly hidden behind a mound of makeup. We had attended church at the ethereal Chapel of the Holy Cross, an architectural wonder completed in 1956 whose entire front glass window gives way to the fantastic rock formations around it, and Tatum had held tight to the cross she wore around her neck. We had eaten ice cream and shopped for trinkets and admired art galleries, and she had given random and very tight hugs, but her sideways glance was often vacant. Despite the radiant sun and warmth of summer, shadows gathered everywhere there, and so my memories of them fell from the first trip across the second.

Nowhere did I sense them more than in the magical passage between the two towns, the fourteen miles of scenic two-way highway from Flagstaff to the overlook at Oak Creek Vista, and the thirteen miles more along Oak Creek Canyon to Sedona. Both times, I felt those shadows that are first the legacy that the original inhabitants, Native Americans—the ancient Sinagua, Yavapai, Apache, to name a few—left upon the land. When the first White settlers arrived, they found and took over remnants of planted crops and orchards, which they gladly claimed for themselves. The shadows also called me to regard the soul, spirit and sorrow of people who have left a lasting imprint, vanished, and are rising again. Native crafts, trading posts and traditions can be found everywhere along this route, and Native Americans and tourists gather in large numbers at the overlook in good weather.

But my second trip was also overlaid with other shadows, those of Tatum and our time together there. After our family visit ended, and her parents and siblings went home, my husband and I had a whole extra day to spend with her alone. What she chose for us to do was to take the road from Sedona through Oak Creek Canyon to Flagstaff and back.

First entering that twisting road through forests of Ponderosa pine, oak, sycamore and walnut trees, overseen sometimes by towering red rock formations, we followed the turns of the clear, inviting water of Oak Creek as it flows toward the Verde River, and I felt the power of renewal. The water that, even despite drought, runs eternally over the smooth stones, the forests that regenerate every year, the sky that never fails to cover all with its protective dome—surely, I thought, such embracing beauty, such unspoken power would give Tatum the strength to heal, and me the courage to hope. We remained silent, the three of us, and when I glanced at her, I felt she was experiencing what I was.

When we reached Flagstaff, we parked near downtown and walked around a few blocks where Tatum had previously been with her mother. She became a chatty, affectionate teenager, who was happy browsing for trinkets and found a café she wanted us to settle in. There by a wide window looking out at the town, she spoke openly about some of her experiences, her pain, and her hopes for the future. She wanted to reunite with her family, to go back to school and get good grades, to look to a life beyond that, even to a career that was not her previous preference—to be an influencer on Tik-Tok. My spirits lifted on the light breeze; then we crossed the street and they fell as the wind fell. Suddenly the girl who had just laid out a future that was predicated on a clean bill of health was excitedly drawn to a head shop filled with glass bongs, vapes and other drug paraphernalia. She tugged my hand to let her go in, and I insisted she was too young. Still, it was clear from her interest—and her knowledge—she was a frightening familiar in this territory.

On the return trip, back to Sedona through the canyon that I had hoped would be her—our—road to redemption, she was silent again, but I glimpsed the blankness that seized her face sometimes, and felt the dark shadows fall on mine. I also replayed shards of disturbing conversation, about forbidden contact with a boyfriend, about admired friends who had run away.

Back in town, we again visited a trading post near a favored ice cream shop, and spoke about the church with the glass window, making it seem there was no separation between the building and the the rocks and canyon below. It was, we both agreed, a special way to approach God, close perhaps to the way the Native Americans approached the Creator. Then it was time to return her to her school in a dusty and dry patch on hilly land south of town. She gave us last hugs and assured us she was doing fine and was feeling so much better, then ran to be greeted by a group of girls.

Of course what she said is what I—what all of us—wanted fervently to believe. But as anyone who has waited heartsick by a phone, or on a darkening night, or in a hospital waiting room for a missing child to return knows, the road to redemption is long. I now understand that just as the café and headshop are my most indelible memories of Flagstaff, as the Chapel of the Holy Cross and the ice cream shop are of Sedona, the transformative hope I felt driving Oak Creek Canyon was not false; it was just delayed. During our trip there with Tatum, we were actually on the road to redemption, and her eventual recovery *would* come through a profound interaction with nature and beauty, but from there we could not see the whole itinerary. Though there have been many highs and lows and many stops along the way, I believe now we have closed the door on that part of the journey. The first trip between Flagstaff and Sedona through Oak Creek Canyon was an important part of it. For that I remain immensely grateful.

The author in her beloved desert

Step by Step at the Grand Staircase-Escalante
Tatum Tomlinson

During the winter of 2022-2023 I lived in the Grand Staircase-Escalante, a national monument 8,600 feet high in the desert of southern Utah. Not just near the monument, but in it. For seventeen weeks, my home was the juniper trees, the pink, the gray, and the white mountains, the sandy dirt on the ground and the sage bushes surrounding me. I was relieved to arrive after the exhausting trip, even though I was unsure what to expect. I had been in so many other programs with little result, my parents had enrolled me in a wilderness therapy program called WinGate.

Imagine a girl, one who's bitter, stubborn and angry on the outside, all in layers so thick that anyone who didn't know her might think there's nothing underneath. But just past the wall she's built is a pit of hurt and hopelessness, one that's so deep nothing has been able to fill it. That's a quick summary of the girl I was when I showed up in snow late one night in October, not exactly sure how I was supposed to get by on what seemed like so little. I couldn't help but have my doubts that this extreme experience would make a difference.

The program was structured so there were specific groups for adolescent boys, girls, one for adults. The handful of girls in our group were accompanied by two trained counselors we called Wind-Walkers (the wind that shapes the trees—the students—into what they become). We lived outside for eight to twelve weeks and survived on the basic necessities: food, sleeping bags, and the clothing on our backs. We even carved our own eating utensils out of tree branches! We were supplied with only the very basics, so we had to turn to each other, and the land we stood, slept, ate, loved and lived on. While I was in the desert, I made the best friends I've ever had, and we still put in effort to see each other regularly, no matter how much it takes.

Even with the repetition of our daily schedule of eating, packing, hiking, unpacking, cooking and falling asleep, even though I missed a warm bed, my favorite foods, the things I comforted and distracted myself with, and most of all my family, I seldom felt unhappy. I believe there were a few things that contributed to this, but the factor from which I genuinely flourished was the nature surrounding us.

I've never believed that any words could fully describe my relationship with the desert, or even come close, and although I've tried my best, there was something about the dirt in my nails and the smoke on my skin, the scent of fire being made or of wet sage, and the array of colors, shapes and textures that were in constant change everywhere I looked, that could not be replicated without direct experience. The coyotes howling late at night and the wind blowing through the trees, these things were only a fraction of what makes the desert what it is. I can't count the number of times I have cried from the sensational beauty of it all, its beauty not just being in the sights you see but in what you hear, taste, touch, smell and breathe. When I say "the desert," "the land," or anything of the sort, *that* is what I am talking about. Not just the ground or the trees, but everything that was there and everything it made me feel. It is all the wonderful things and they have all been there for a very long time, all of them put there by our Earth, our God, or whatever/whoever one believes has been here from the beginning.

The things that make the desert beautiful are all natural, not man-made like so many of the everyday things we rely on. Out in the Grand Staircase, we were cared for by the resources that land provided, and we depended solely on the land to survive. It wasn't a choice, but when I learned that nothing had ever made me feel as secure as the desert did, I couldn't turn back. It became my home, and I would do anything to protect it the way that it cared for me. Without its resources, we wouldn't have had a bed of duff under a juniper tree to keep us from freezing at night or the wood we needed to build fires that fed us. We would never have gotten to experience sliding down cliffs of sand and clay or having the last sight of the day, just before closing our eyes, being the stars above us, looking hundreds of times brighter than they ever did back in the city. Some of the things the desert gave us, we didn't even need, but we loved them. Sometimes it was just pure joy, and sometimes it was excruciating pain. I remember lying on the snow for many of those nights, with nothing but a sleeping bag in weather that was so freezing we couldn't sleep, just so that the next day would feel that much better. The desert pushed me to be grateful and to see the best in everything.

While I was staying in the Grand Staircase, the power of that wild place, as well as the support from many people in my life, allowed me to experience drastic changes. It took only about a week to feel the hard-hitting impact of the intense detox that is the wilderness, but when it hit, I was unrecognizable. It came in waves, and sure there were bad times, but to this day I have never felt as happy as I did out there. Joyful was the very beginning of the symptoms. Soon I relearned how to become at peace with life, how to take care of myself and then others, how to feel love, how to think through decisions and be honest with myself. I could feel that I was no longer in that pit, and it was a breath of fresh air, long awaited. It actually might have been more like crawling out of a tight, dark space and seeing light for the first time. I was reborn, taking back parts of my personality I had forgotten I even possessed, and then adding new experiences to become even further content with my life.

Being in the desert offers so many benefits that are difficult to find elsewhere. Research shows being in the desert and other similar settings rapidly improves health and mindset, as anyone who has experienced it knows for themselves. For myself, I truly believe that the transformations in my life would not have been so efficient or extreme in any other setting, and the connection I have with the land feels almost predestined. I'm incredibly grateful that fate brought me to the Grand Staircase-Escalante, where I took my first steps on the climb to success. Without that desert experience, I don't have a clue where I'd be today, but I'm positive it would be nowhere close to the person I've become.

Camping in the desert

Borrego Springs' Field of Dreams
Michael J. Fitzgerald

Proximity to water has been the single, unwavering constant in my life.

I grew up on the shore of New York's Lake Chautauqua. Most of my adult life has been spent living in houses with water lapping nearby. The time I have spent in small boats on lakes and large sailing vessels in coastal bays and on oceans can be measured in years. Today I live in a floating home in Oregon moored on a tributary of the mighty Willamette River rushing by to the Pacific.

This life-long aquatic affinity is why visiting the dry Anza-Borrego Desert and town of Borrego Springs gave me such a gut-punching shock.

It felt *instantly* like home.

Not just "like home" but home itself.

It felt as homelike as if I were standing in front of the four-story Brooklyn brownstone I lived in the first nine years of my life until my father died very suddenly, forcing my family to leave the city. It marked the beginning of a life of moving from place to place.

The visit to the Anza-Borrego Desert and Borrego Springs were among the last stops on a seven-day, constant-in-motion writers' retreat/workshop visiting Southern California desert areas that included some pretty strange places populated in large part by some equally eccentric people. My retreat colleagues and I—and our editor-leaders—had been immersed in a swirl of odd vibes thrown at us by the deserts and desert dwellers. Dramatic lighting shifts made landscapes change colors. The weather went from hot-to-cold to cold-to-hot and the minimalist desert culture at enclaves like Bombay Beach, East Jesus and Salvation Mountain kept us constantly reassessing what we were seeing and hearing.

My going to the deserts was an exercise in curiosity and wanting to stretch my writing muscles. It was the first such writers' retreat/workshop I ever attended after 50 years as a journalist and a decade as a novelist.

The curiosity was sparked in good part by reading tales of the desert mystics, including the Desert Fathers and Mothers. They were among those who went into the desert wilderness 300-plus years after the birth of Christ, founding small communities based on lives of strict asceticism and eschewing even simple comforts. The communities were the beginnings of the Christian monasteries that later became fixtures across Europe.

A Catholic priest mentor told me that while deserts described in most biblical writings portray a dangerous landscape filled with death, they also were—and are—places where mystical revelations abound and spiritual growth can erupt suddenly.

Mystical revelations and desert-inspired leaps of spiritual growth are not usually associated with journalists. But something about the lives of these early Christians gave me an added push to join the small band of travel writers making organized forays into the desert.

Driving into the Anza-Borrego on our third day, we followed well-traveled roads and footpaths trampled by tourists. We pulled over at a vast field of flowers, startled to see the bright colors across miles and miles of sand and sagebrush as we drove in. The flowers were an early desert bloom fueled by record California rainfalls. Purple, yellow and orange flowers stretched to the base of mountains miles away. The fields held the promise of more blooms under the sandy soil. As we wandered and photographed, the phrase "field of dreams" popped into my head, the title of a popular 1989 movie by that name.

Like a musical earworm, it stuck.

We eventually drove on from the desert flowers to a sandy area with acres and acres of scrub brush and sand dunes called Galleta Meadows. There we went face-to-face with huge metal sculptures scattered about. Some depicted dinosaurs and other monster-like creations.

The sculptures were built between 2008 and 2012 by artist Ricardo Breceda. He had been commissioned to create them by landowner and Borrego Valley resident Dennis Avery, who reportedly got the idea for the sculptures via a now-well-known 2006 book about the fossils studied by paleontologists: *Fossil Treasures of the Anza Borrego Desert*.

The contrast between the acres of vivid flowers and the sculptures was stark. The sculptures invoked nearly equal measures of awe at the artistry and mild uneasiness at the representations of velociraptors and other creatures.

Sure, these metal sculptures are just shaped tin and steel, the work of a talented mind, but still. I heard campers talking about where to spend the night among the monster artworks. That made me wonder about camping there after nightfall, pondering what it would be like when it turned cold and real-life desert denizens began scurrying about. A sculpture of a giant scorpion attacking an equally large grasshopper reminded me that real scorpions with real poisonous stingers were lurking in the brush.

The dinosaurs and other monster-like sculptures draw much of the attention of tourists who flock to the Borrego Springs area annually. In winter the town of 3,000 residents swells to 10,000. But there are plenty of less-intimidating, powerful representations of people and events among the 130 sculptures placed around Borrego Springs. Breceda showed his genius creating sculptures like one of Captain Juan Bautista, who opened the first road into California in 1774. Another piece shows a gold miner and his mule reminding of the transformation to California by the gold rush in the 1840s. A sculpture of farmworkers in a field graphically illustrates the struggles of migrant workers who once toiled in the Borrego Valley harvesting grapes. Along with other California farmworkers, they went on strike and fought a five-year battle that ended up in the courts.

What I was seeing and experiencing in the desert in Borrego was information-stimulation overload that I tried to make sense of like a good journalist.

But that day in Anza-Borrego and Borrego Springs I surrendered my good-journalist approach. It was clear I needed to lean less on decades of objective journalistic examination and instead view these deserts and everything about them more like a painter, less like a photographer.

Our entourage reluctantly left the sculptures and sand dunes to make its way into the actual village of Borrego Springs nearby, a bustling place with plenty of tourists and touristy shops. But it felt more authentic, less smarmy and imported than tourist venues like Pier 39 in San Francisco. The Borrego Springs shopkeepers and museum staff seemed sincere in their desire to ensure customers got just the right sculpture map, clever post card or desert-related gizmo.

They proudly touted that it's the only town in California completely surrounded by a state park and is an official International Dark Sky Community dedicated to protecting the night sky from light pollution, one of only a few in California.

Over lunch at a highly recommended Mexican restaurant, we swapped stories about travels to other locales and what we had seen among the flowers, dunes, sculptures and the sand town civilization. Then we split up for a last look before heading back to our Palm Springs basecamp hotel.

I walked alone to the edge of town to peer off into the Anza-Borrego Desert that stretched to the horizon. Even with a high overcast, the desert air still shimmered from heat. I wondered about living there in the winter when the weather is amenable and not beastly hot. It seemed absurdly far-fetched until the feeling of home popped up again. It was that comfortable, familiar feeling—like making the last few driving turns in your neighborhood before pulling up in front of your house.

I didn't want to leave.

I walked quickly back to the real estate office I had seen earlier and asked about RV parks, camping and property for sale. A clerk offered advice about inexpensive vacant sand lots for sale where no development was contemplated.

I flirted with the idea of buying a desert lot on the spot. It would be a place to park my travel trailer on future visits, maybe even build some small desert home.

Home.

Then I remembered the best-known line from the film *Field of Dreams*.

"If you build if *he* will come."

Cripes.

All my life I have unconsciously waited for my long-deceased father to somehow stroll back into my life. Why couldn't he just walk out of the desert like a long-lost mystic? I shook my head and wondered exactly how much tequila had been in my lunchtime margarita as I hurried to join my writer amigos. I was oddly fearful of looking behind me into the desert as I walk-ran to our vehicles.

I had come to these deserts to find something. Borrego Springs showed me I needed to come back.

And keep looking.

A vast expanse of sand and silence
at White Sands National Monument

WHITE SANDS AND SILENCE
Naomi Lopez

A sudden pain in my leg pulls me out of a deep focus. I had been gazing out the window at the vast expanse of desert and towering Sacramento Mountains beyond. I face forward as I attempt to stretch out my spontaneous hamstring cramp. Grant sits hunched over in the driver's seat, his fluffy blond hair brushing the roof of the car. Alexis leans curiously out of the passenger window, her long black curls blowing in the wind. "Let's Be Still" plays over the quiet hum of the engine as we make our way down the winding road.

As my cramp subsides, I look over at the mess of supplies piled next to me in the backseat. I assume my designated role of sandwich maker and begin assembling PB&Js. It's only the second day of our road trip—the first was spent driving ten hours on the I-10 west across West Texas to New Mexico—but we've already watched the sunrise at Carlsbad Caverns and hiked through Lincoln National Forest. We're in desperate need of fuel for the next half of our day. The familiar scent of peanut butter and jelly soon permeates the car as we drive along the never-ending horizon of desert mountains toward our next destination: White Sands

National Park, located at the northern end of the Chihuahuan Desert in New Mexico.

It was spring of 2021. Alexis, Grant and I had met in the dorms our freshman year at UCLA. We led normal college freshman lives—we partied, we studied, we became close friends without really knowing each other—until the Pandemic hit halfway through the year. Though we all returned to Westwood sophomore year, things weren't the same. There was the occasional hangout, but for the most part, an unspoken longing for a sense of connectedness seemed to pervade the months leading up to spring. After a year of online classes, confinement to the indoors and academic stress, my fellow introverted friends and I craved nothing more than a humble escape to the outdoors. Most of our peers looked forward to spending their spring break drinking all day on a tropical island, but the idea never enticed us. A road trip, we decided, was necessary.

We finish our sandwiches just as we pull into the parking lot. I'm suddenly blinded by a bright light pouring in from outside. Confused, I blink rapidly and let my eyes adjust.

Dozens of white sand dunes surround us on every side. Some are tall, piled high into the clear blue sky, with children sledding down them. The sun shines relentlessly, casting its warmth like a blanket over the sand and reflecting its light back up. Countless families with young children, visitors just like us, frolic around the area. Sand toys are strewn about, and buzzing conversations and cheerful shouts fill the air.

The three of us hop out of the car and seamlessly join the large group of scattered guests. Alexis lays a blanket on the closest sand dune, and she and I stretch out across it. I put on my sunglasses, close my eyes and soak in the sunlight in silence.

It feels like the happy and chaotic yet calm embrace of a summer beach day when you were a child. The tangible excitement of being in a new place, most likely on vacation with your family, and taking in a completely new landscape. Lounging lazily under the sun without a care in the world. Not a thought about school or the future. Simply present with those around you.

Grant wanders several yards away from our set-up, digging curiously around the sand. He suddenly kicks at a small pile, and a white flurry of sand flies up into the air. I smirk to myself at his childlike behavior and look over to see if Alexis has noticed, but she's preoccupied with a ladybug crawling slowly up her forearm.

She sees me looking over and silently passes the ladybug to me. I put it down and watch it intently, each of its tiny legs taking calculated, effortful steps across every grain of sand.

After several more minutes of this—Grant playing, Alexis lounging, me entertaining myself with the ladybug—we decide to get up and explore more.

"There are a few hikes we can do," Grant says. "This one's an easy two-miler out and back, and this one's a five-mile loop," he adds, pointing to the map he brought with him.

"If we're here we might as well do the longer one," I say with a shrug.

They both nod in agreement and we set off, deeper into the dunes and away from the sounds.

The laughter and voices slowly fade away as we make our way farther from the main lot. Soon enough, all we can see around us are towering white sand dunes against a perfectly blue sky.

We stop a few times to take pictures, mostly to capture Grant's hiking attire. He sports his infamous black hoodie and black sweats, but a T-shirt now covers his entire head and nearly all of his face. With the addition of a pair of sunglasses, only his hands are visible.

"So I don't get sunburnt," he says matter-of-factly.

Our own laughs and conversation fizzle out as we settle into the quiet of the hike. There's no one else around. The sun lowers gradually and the breeze picks up, but we carry on unbothered. After a while, I notice that the only sounds are the occasional gusty wind against the side of my head or the ruffle of my shirt in the breeze.

I pause suddenly.

"What is it?" Alexis asks. She and Grant stop walking.

"Wait, stop for a second and turn this way," I say, twisting slightly to my left so the wind doesn't blow into the side of my head.

They follow suit wordlessly.

"I don't know if I've ever heard silence like this before," I say with awe. It might be silent when I'm in bed or at a library, but never have I been outdoors and heard complete silence. There are always sirens, voices, cars, even birds or bugs. But this is true silence. With the wind blocked from my ear, it's as if someone has put the world on mute.

I continue to stand motionlessly, reveling in this novel experience.

The blue sky has lightened a few shades, the sun has dimmed slightly and a few wispy clouds have appeared. The white sand appears darker now that the sun reflects much less of its light. I can feel the cold air push against me, but it's a silent force. I take in a deep breath of fresh air and try to remember as much detail as I can about this moment. It feels like one that I will wish to recall later on.

In my periphery, I see Alexis and Grant standing still, listening intently to the nothingness. I consider moving on; I don't want to hurry the group, especially if they're as taken by this moment as I am. With different friends, we would have been walking along minutes ago. But I suddenly realize that Grant and Alexis are the type of not just friends, but people who also enjoy these moments. An involuntary grin spreads across my face as the realization sinks in.

After a bit longer, we continue on. My legs are starting to feel heavy, but an unconscious, newfound energy seems to make my arms swing more and my feet pick up higher off the sand. I notice a similar shift in Alexis and Grant.

Sunset approaches seemingly faster and faster, and we're still about a mile out.

"Should we just watch it from the top of one of these mountains?" Alexis suggests.

Grant and I agree and start climbing up one of the taller sand dunes near us. We slow as we reach the top, the fatigue from two hours of hiking under the sun fully setting in. We collapse on the sand, sitting crisscross applesauce beside each other.

Across the large, flat valley of sand down below, the great yellow-orange ball makes its trip downward, retiring for the day behind another eye-level sand dune. A light yellow tint on the horizon blends slowly into a pastel green and finally a light blue as the sun disappears fully from view.

A quiet, pensive contentment radiates among us.

"I think we should each play our favorite songs," Alexis says suddenly, breaking the silence.

I play the song "Saturn" by Sleeping at Last. I quickly blink away the tears that fill my eyes at the sound of my favorite lyrics: "How rare and beautiful it is to even exist ... the universe was made just to be seen by my eyes."

"That was beautiful," Alexis remarks as the song ends.

White, wispy clouds shift slowly into shades of light pinks and purples, coloring the ever-fading light blue sky.

"I'm really glad we decided to go on this road trip," Grant says, looking out at the waning sunlight.

"Yeah, me too," I say quietly, nodding in agreement.

None of us are the type to verbally express our emotions to each other on the spot, especially in a moment as intimate as this one. But just these few comments are enough to capture our shared sentiment of gratitude for one another and for the experiences we've had. Words aren't really necessary. It's understood implicitly.

With no need for additional exchange, we sit there in near silence. Music plays softly from Alexis's phone, and I can hear the gentle breeze against my ears. A deep sense of gratitude overcomes me again. I feel grateful for friends with whom I can exist in silence without it being uncomfortable. Grateful for friends who silently appreciate nature the same way I do. Grateful for friends who can sit and enjoy silence itself with me.

We make it back to the car just as dusk settles in. I'm in the passenger's seat this time. Grant hands Alexis and me an apple each from the backseat as we set off down the barren, black road.

My mind wanders once again. A calm, peaceful feeling that I can't quite decipher settles over me. I feel appreciative of the sights I've seen, and the particular feelings and experiences one can only get from immersing oneself in nature. This solace from the outdoors is precisely what we all hoped to find on this trip after being holed up indoors all winter long. Needless to say, we were successful.

Beyond that, though, there's another layer to the tranquility I feel. After several minutes replaying the day's events in my head, I finally identify it: a sense of connectedness. Through both the ordinary and unique moments with my friends—enjoying the sun, hiking in silence, appreciating a sunset—I've found a sort of congruence I had been lacking for months.

Marveling at the deeply connective power nature holds, I lean out the window and rest my chin on my forearm. My gaze once again fixes on the scene beyond: the dark layer of purple setting on the horizon, the distant desert mountains fading from view.

Life is a game of chance when you're on the lam with Mean Vick.

POETIC JUSTICE
Judy Zimola

Mean Vick and I are on the lam. Skedaddled. Vamoosed. Amscrayed. January woke up pissy this morning, her skies dense and gray as this stretch of I-80 that's running under the Jeep's tires. It's eight hours east to our destination: Elko, Nevada's Cowboy Poetry Festival.

Hunkered down in the high desert of western Nevada, Elko is an excellent outpost for those absconding. Long sweeps of scrubby sage roll for miles as the horizon shifts colors like a peevish mood ring, turning from blue-black to slate. Daybreak tries to push past the heavy clouds, only to be met by the crossed arms of low hills, bristling with snow and shale.

Sleet peppers the windshield as wipers spank their backbeat to my jangling thoughts. "Bad person, bad person," they thump. When the rain slackens and a little squeak enters the beat, they *nyah-nyah* me like kids on a schoolyard blacktop: "You're SO screwed. You're SO screwed."

Vick, on the other hand, is in her element. Feet on the dash, sucking Smarties and looking out the window, she's a study in serenity. By turns I'm frightened, inspired and impressed by her utter lack of remorse. When it comes to dealing out retribution,

Mean Vick is the most innovative person I've ever known—Jackson Pollock wielding a paint brush full of "bite me." Early in our friendship, I watched her methodically fill out and mail subscription requests to a couple dozen magazines in the name of her ex-boyfriend. "Should I really send *Knitter's Monthly*? Oh hell, why not?" she snorted, dropping the last No-Postage-Required flyer into the mailbox.

Nothing less than her patented brand of "goddam" would do for my situation: a love gone so far south it's wearing a serape. Over black and tans late one winter night at a bar in San Francisco's Mission District, she spelled out the plan. With every detail it became clear that she had crafted not another saucy little scheme, but a fully realized opus: malfeasant, rhythmic, layered with wit and vitriol. The victim (my cheating boyfriend) would experience tics, trauma and nightmares as a result of this act. It was a nasty, bitchy thing to do. God help me, I loved it.

Not only am I screwed, I'm a screwed sociopath.

"Ooh, a coffee shop!" Vick is pointing out the window at a mom-and-pop diner. If she had a tail, it would be thumping against the console. "Let's get waffles!"

"Vick," I say, pulling into Red's Waffle Hut, "I feel kinda funny about, you know, what we did. To Steve."

She pretends not to hear. "I hope they make them crispy. I hate a limp waffle."

"We just left him there, Vick. He twitched. We saw it."

"Dammit, Judy, stop being such a drama queen," Vick demands. "Steve had it coming. No regrets. No looking back."

"Can you throw one more cliché at this?"

"There's lots of fish in the sea? It's better to have loved and lost? You want clichés, sister, I got a bag of them right here."

I really hate her sometimes.

Coffee that takes the enamel off my teeth and a plate of corned beef hash help shift my perspective. It's still drizzling as we climb back in the Jeep, but that's good. The rain, mixed with the cold air's metallic smell, puts everything into sharp relief. I-80's stark landscape has a kind of steel wool effect, scouring my muzzy core.

Half past Winnemucca, rain turns to snow; giant flakes splat icy guts across the windshield like polar Junebugs. About an hour west of Elko the Ruby Mountains rise up from the desert; Vick leans against the passenger door as if to snuggle into its he-man contours. "I wonder if we'll see Jason White Feather."

Oh yes, Jason White Feather. Vick is a pushover for Crow Indian poets from Montana with cool hair and mystique; Mr. White Feather has been on Vick's radar for weeks. Consequently, White Feather updates are part of my daily news diet. JWF works at a school in admissions; JWF lives with his dad; a dreamy, four-color photo of JWF standing by a Montana stream was just published in a poetry anthology. "He wears a ponytail, you know."

Do I know. "Yeah, you told me. So?"

"So, it'll make it easier for me to drag him around."

Slushy snow is still coming down as we pull into the parking lot of the EZ Sleep Motel in Elko. It's not a bad place—for a fleabag—just misunderstood. There are your standard doubles with brown quilts, backache no extra charge, bark cloth curtains over a window looking directly into the grille of a Dodge pickup truck, a clanking radiator emitting dusty-smelling steam heat. The sight of the heavy black rotary dial phone with a silver finger-stopper rips a serrated shiver straight between my shoulder blades. Sometime this weekend it's going to ring and it's going to be for me.

I need a drink.

Within the hour, we're in the Stockmen's bar, a good old watering hole redolent of brimming ashtrays and Saturday boot polish. A couple glasses of well whiskey, a twisted best friend who's an ace conspirator, and Hank Williams on the jukebox make this miscreant feel all woolly warm. Especially when I think I recognize . . . "Say, Vick. What did you say Jason White Feather looks like again?"

"Like a Crow Indian with a ponytail." She shakes her head. "Moron."

"Mmmm." I sip my drink and nod toward the end of the bar. "Like maybe, that Crow Indian with the red shirt? I think I'll say hi."

"Oh God." Vick gulps. "It's him. Please don't. Wait. Do. But don't say anything about me. Shit. I have to go to the bathroom."

"Do you want me to talk to him or not?" I may be a moron, but I'll respect her boundaries.

"Sure. But be . . . surreptitious."

So surreptitiously I introduce myself to Jason White Feather while Vick takes a powder. I admire his work, I say, and offer to buy him a beer, which he graciously accepts. Mean Vick returns from the ladies' room, and I see she's applied fresh lipstick.

"Hi," Miss Drag-Him-Around-By-His-Ponytail says, a little breathlessly. "Who's your friend?"

Sly dog. "Vick, meet Jason White Feather. He's a poet."

Vick acts smooth while suppressing hyperventilation, but clinging to the front of her shirt is a white, loosely wadded, dampish glob. "Honey," I murmur, "there's a little something on your, um, your front there."

Confused, she looks down, then gingerly plucks a wad of toilet paper from the front of her new festival blouse. Of the three of us regarding the small, soggy miasma, two of us think it's really damn funny. Mean Vick is mortified. "Happens to me all the time," our new poet pal utters in a voice that's 96 proof. "I'll buy the next round." I notice Vick's not too appalled to request a shot of Maker's Mark and branch water.

A smile skips across Jason White Feather's face, and with a boot-leather hand barely on the small of her back, he guides Mean Vick to the bar. Damn. She's not whistling disco about those Crow Indian poets from Montana—all the ones I've met so far are very sexy. I'm glad, really glad, for Vick. She'll be there for me when we get back home. And thanks to her, my sendoff to Steve was wickedly stylish.

Watching old movies and drinking crappy red wine, Vick and I had taken our time until Steve fell asleep. When his snoring sounded like a clapped-out garbage disposal, it was time to lock and load. I wouldn't allow myself to think about what we were doing. For my sake and the sake of all womanhood, this had to be seen through. As we continued the grim task, Steve convulsed and threw his hand behind his head. Mean Vick barely paused before going back to it. I began to giggle helplessly.

"*Finish* it," Vick hissed.

Squashed snorts augured my nasal passages, filling my eyes. "I will. You finish!"

Wielding brushes laden with Revlon's classic "Love That Red," Mean Vick and I stroked swaths of scarlet on Steve's fingernails. We allowed just a moment to admire our work before sidling out the front door and into the inky Frisco streets, getaway Jeep packed and ready. On the bathroom sink, like a big, upraised middle finger, we left a bottle of fingernail polish remover—empty.

He did have it coming. I'll have to start over after this weekend, and that's going to suck. But right now, sipping whiskey with Vick—Jason White Feather and Elko as our inamoratos—the ending is in every way, poetry.

Ruins at Wijiji

CHACO CANYON:
A DESERT REDEMPTION

J. R. Barnett

In 2008 I found myself out of work at the inception of the largest economic bust since the Great Depression. I'd been an executive at a Silicon Valley software company for the preceding ten years, commuting 180 miles round trip each day from my home north of the Golden Gate to San Jose, working six days per week, twelve hours per day. When the company was acquired by a larger company, I stuck around for six months to help integrate my employer's sales and technology development functions into the acquiring company, then proceeded to sit on the couch at home for several weeks, numb. I was burned out, and with some breathing room courtesy of unexpected unemployment checks, became aware of how much actual living I'd missed while chasing economic gain.

I'd not always been a "suit." I had many work-a-day jobs in my youth: janitor, delivery driver, fry cook, feed mill worker, beer brewer and wheat farmer. At university, I studied things that interested me: history, classics and anthropology. I learned Latin and

Ancient Greek and taught myself a smattering of Sanskrit along the way. I'd wanted to be an archaeologist since I was eight years old, but as I gained the skills useful for making that a reality, I was advised by father, teachers, professors and friends that I would likely starve and that archaeologists were little more than "ditch diggers." So, I sold out and went to law school, which eventually led to in-house senior legal positions at several large technology companies.

After only two weeks of sitting around the house, I concluded that I needed some kind of redemption and renewal—or even a rebirth. I wanted to reconnect with the things that had inspired and awed me when I was younger, and re-learn how to observe, experience and interact with others in the broader world outside of the sterile, rules-laden, greed-fueled corporate environment. But how?

I am a nerd with a capital "N." Among my many nerdy hobbies and interests, astronomy occupies a high place. In a dream one night I recalled a place I'd seen in the 1980s series *Cosmos*. I had a mind's-eye view of looking down from atop a cliff over a sprawling and strange D-shaped stone ruin peppered with many different-sized circular walled structures within its perimeter. The next day I purchased the original *Cosmos* series on Apple TV and started watching from the first episode to find the segment I'd dreamed about. Episode 3, "Harmony of Worlds," contained what I was looking for. The place was located in northwest New Mexico and called Chaco Canyon. More properly known as Chaco Canyon National Historical Park, it is near the Navajo Nation town of Crownpoint north of Gallup.

After a bit of online research about the canyon and its history, I loaded up my Subaru with camping and astronomy gear that I hadn't used in a decade and set out for Chaco. My poor car was beat up and tired. More than one thousand commuting miles per week tends to do that. Unsurprisingly, it overheated climbing the Tehachapi Grade. I remedied this malady by running the heater full blast, despite the high 90s exterior temperature, and coasted down the back side using only light throttle. After descending, I pulled into a rest stop near Mojave, California, and topped up the radiator overflow tank with one of the precious few bottles of ice-cold drinking water from the cooler. Many more hours of driving, followed by one mediocre delivery pizza and four hours of restless, fitful sleep in a run-down roadside motel in Flagstaff, then back on the road to Chaco at sun-up, left me anxious to get there and start my quest to find the "me" that had gone missing.

The demarcation between the desert I'd crossed the day before, the Mojave, and the desert I was entering approaching the Arizona-New Mexico border, the Colorado Plateau, was startling and sudden. The beiges and tans of the sandy, chaparral-choked Mojave gave way to the fractured, terra-cotta-toned sandstone cliffs of the Colorado Plateau. As I barreled along the interstate, welcomed by thunderheads emerging over the red rock cliffs to the north and a "Welcome to New Mexico" sign ahead, it felt as if a great weight were lifted from my shoulders. At last I wasn't running away from, but rather *to*, something.

Turning north through Gallup, New Mexico, and Diné country, home of "The People" and what is often called "the heart of the Navajo Nation," I drove past lonely trailers, weathered manufactured homes, empty corrals and desiccated pastures supporting sad-looking flocks of sheep. I passed defunct trading posts, their faded, once brightly hued signs recalling better days. Then the route began to climb through broken hills dotted with sparse trees and jagged sandstone outcrops. I arrived at the small town of Crownpoint and refueled. There would be no services—no gasoline, no ice, no groceries, *nada*—within two hours' drive of Chaco Canyon. This was it: the last civilization I would see for the coming two weeks.

There are two routes into the canyon, a North Road and a South Road. Neither is paved. Neither is in very good condition. The North Road is slightly better maintained, being graded every other year, but when approaching Chaco Canyon from the south, the Gallup side, going around to the North Road represents a longer, more circuitous route, so I took the South Road. Either route is passable with care in an ordinary passenger car, unless it has rained recently, in which case the sandstone dust that lines the ruts turns into a slippery-sticky desert toffee, making progress difficult, but with high clearance and all-wheel-drive or a true dual-range 4x4, you'll generally make it through.

The South Road leaves BIA-9 and meanders eighteen miles north over rolling cattle land before returning to pavement at the park's south boundary. I encountered a guardian spirit at mile nine. It took the menacing form of a black long-horned bull standing in the road facing the car. What does one do about moving an ill-tempered 800-pound horned animal out of the way? Very little, it turns out. I didn't honk. I didn't crowd the bull with my bumper. I certainly didn't get out. I waited patiently. So did the bull. After a half hour of this nonsensical behavior, the bull tossed its horns from side to side in defiance and wandered away. Chaco had weighed me and granted entrance.

I approached the park's southern boundary, driving toward a gap in a craggy, brooding mesa, crowned with towering stratocumulus. The South Road entered the canyon through a narrow cleft in this mesa, called South Mesa. I passed Fajada Butte to my right. From the *Cosmos* vignette I knew that this was the location of the famous "Sun Dagger" site, a solstice, equinox and lunar cycle calendaring device. I crossed the canyon south to north, stopping at the visitor's center where I met the rangers, checked in and payed the park entrance fee. Unlike most park properties with cultural or archeological sites, Chaco doesn't offer ranger-led walks. Visits to the ruins, rock art sites and the rest are entirely self-led affairs.

Heading east along the park's main road I came to Gallo Campground. It was mostly empty. I set up my tent, rolled out my sleeping gear, deployed the astronomy equipment and booted up for a sunset hike to my first Chacoan great house ruin, Wijiji. The route to Wijiji followed a narrow two-track fire road from the campground, around a mesa spur to the southeast, and off eastward along the eastern branch of Chaco Canyon. After a mile and a half of mostly flat walking, Fajada Butte blazed red behind me in the feeble rays of the sun as it dipped behind South Mesa. I saw an otherworldly site ahead in the purplish gloom: Wijiji.

Wijiji is a precisely laid out rectangular pueblo. Its long axis, at fifty-three meters, is aligned east-west and backs up to the north canyon wall overhang. It is fashioned of meticulously stacked, precisely worked slabs of tabular sandstone on both exterior and interior sides of its walls, with a rubble-filled core in between. Wijiji is bilaterally symmetrical and contains approximately 100 rooms and two kivas: circular, subterranean spaces used for rituals and ceremonies. Even in shadow the craft of the masonry is apparent; the builders deliberately banded the walls with alternating dark and light sandstone blocks. This is puzzling, given that when Chaco's great house structures were occupied, the walls were sheathed in white plaster, inside and out. This stone artistry would have been invisible to anyone but the masons who originally built it.

I explored the intricate maze-like chambers of roofless Wijiji and circumambulated its exterior perimeter as full darkness engulfed the ruin. Lacking an artificial light source, I stumbled haltingly back toward camp. As night settled over the canyon and my eyes gradually adapted, I was surprised to detect a faint, ghostly light from above. I looked up and saw that my way was lit by the glow of two billion suns making up the lumpy, mottled band of the summer Milky Way. It was so primordially dark that the cloud of our home galaxy's stars actually cast my shadow on the ground.

And just like that I was *me* once more.

The Milky Way glows over a desert archway.

NIGHT SKY
Linda Watanabe McFerrin

It's dusk, and I am sitting quietly just beyond the Orrery, at Sky's the Limit Observatory and Nature Center in Twentynine Palms, California, a campus located in Joshua Tree National Park. This is one of the dozens of locations in the United States that have been designated as "Dark-Sky Preserves," places with starry nights and nocturnal visibility that are specifically protected for scientific, natural, educational, cultural and public enjoyment, and I'm waiting for the stars to come out. It's been a long day, a day of heat, worry and exhaustion and, despite the proximity of the other visitors, I can't help but feel isolated ... isolated and very small and endangered as I sit here in the twilight.

Some yards away, the Orrery—a model of the solar system named after Charles Boyle, the fourth Earl of Orrery, who is credited with commissioning the first proportional representation of this kind—stretches into the distance in a true-to-scale, twenty-billion-to-one replication of our solar system. I've had many night sky adventures in the past, but this is different. In those, I was simply an observer. Here, in Joshua Tree, on this particular night, I seem to have lost that status. I feel as if there is no separation, no safe space between me and everything around me ... everything *out there*.

This evening, it seems, we have all drifted toward our own murky horizons. I'm with a group of writers, each in their own world, every one of us on a different adventure. I might as well be in outer space.

Our day began in the same space: Pappy & Harriet's Pioneertown Palace, a legendary roadhouse around ten miles from Joshua Tree National Park. This popular restaurant-bar-music venue, a made-for-movies cantina that later became Pappy & Harriet's, is located on a property—Pioneertown—that has served as a Western-style movie set for filmmakers since the 1940s. Pappy & Harriet's has been serving up music and food since the '70s when Harriet's mother purchased it. Since then, and despite changes in ownership, it's been an off-the-usual-menu venue for some of the planet's top-rated performers. Paul McCartney, Lucinda Williams, Robert Plant, Tanya Tucker, Patti Smith, The Dead Kennedys, and other world-famous headliners have graced its small stage. I love the Wild West atmosphere, the jeans-and-boots vibe of the place. Mostly, I enjoy pulling up to a restaurant where a signature string of motorcycles lines up in front like so many horses tied to a hitching post. I always have a great time at Pappy & Harriet's, but on this morning, one of our company has grown faint, reacting maybe to the sizeable portions, the drink, the heat or the exhaustion of too many much-too-long days of running around in the hot desert sun. What is clear right away is that this traveler needs to slow down. A few questions later I know why. Our companion has recently experienced an affair of the heart ... by that I mean a situation where stress tests and heart monitors were involved.

Night Sky — Linda Watanabe McFerrin

Having just emerged from a similar experience—maybe induced by the recently debilitating Pandemic, maybe by the death of my younger and last sibling in a hospital where no one could visit him, maybe by my own long-term heart issues—I am deeply concerned. When the situation worsens visibly (pale appearance, dizziness, some confusion) Lowry, who has been trained in lifesaving procedures, recommends rest and certainly NOT another pitiless day in the desert heat that won't end until long after nightfall. Stressed, but not as stressed as our fading companion, we insist on taking our car, making the drive back to headquarters or maybe even to a hospital, depending on what transpires as we hustle our friend to safety.

On the sixty-mile drive back to headquarters, my own heart pounding, the stress of pandemic loss, too many illnesses, too many bad decisions, too much bad governance and far too many untimely deaths is weighing heavily upon me. Our friend refuses an emergency room visit and, as the symptoms seem to be subsiding, we agree that more water, a lie-down and a well-monitored rest with emergency transport close at hand will do. Once our passenger is safely tucked in a bedroom, we, too, take a much-needed breather, waiting until we are one hundred percent certain that all is well before departing to rejoin the others and resume that day's desert expedition. By then it is late, dinner long over, and we have not been able to reach our group, though we tried several times. We drive through the thickening darkness to Sky's the Limit Observatory and Nature Center, our end-of-day destination, arriving exhausted, still a bit worried, still wrapped up in the utter unpredictability of our lives, the impossibility of ensuring our own—or anyone's—safety, the worry, the sorrow, the sense of loss that has darkened our world through the past months and years of

Pandemic. I'm looking forward to a heavenly sparkle, a jet-black sky a-twinkle with stars ... but no, this night, it seems, a sinister fog has wrapped us in a hazy twilight, cottony but cool, that masks the heavens, absorbs almost all sound and makes breathing ... even thinking ... difficult.

In this state there is no elation. We get no jolly greetings. Our once-cheerful band of travelers seems even more somber than us. The long distances suggested by the Orrery contribute to a feeling of isolation so vast, I feel as though I am drifting through space where the lack of an atmosphere has gobbled up joy. We are not even able to view the night sky. A low-hanging haze prevents stargazing. COVID precludes group use of the dome's Schmidt-Cassegrain telescope. It is a contemplative and introspective gathering that makes its way to the picnic tables adjacent to the non-functioning telescope for the planned lecture.

By this time, it is dark, extremely cold, and getting colder by the minute. We all, our small party and the many others assembled, sit hunched at picnic tables as the astronomer, Darrell Shade, sets up a laptop and announces that although we cannot see the stars through the thick curtain of mist, we'll be viewing a slide show on screen and listening to a lecture. I am reminded of the darkened rooms of my school days, when the lights were turned out and a commentator, teacher or professor droned on. But as we all huddle closer, like herd animals seeking warmth and reassurance, as deep sky image after image of a universe studded with stars explodes on the screen before us, something happens. We are transported, taken to distant planets, stars, constellations, nebulas, galaxies, some up as many as twenty-three and forty-six million light years away. Galaxies: Whirlpool, Sunflower, Black Eye, Crab, Star and Cigar swirl before us. Stars: binary, double cluster, beehive cluster, open cluster and globular cluster glitter. Nebulas: Cone, Orion, Horsehead, Crab and Red Flame light up the dark screen. When one considers that one light year is equivalent to "around" *six trillion* miles, the cosmic dimension of this extravaganza is mind-blowing. Suddenly I feel very small ... but also very safe, very happy in my role as no more than an infinitesimal bit of a much larger body. And, strangely, I am actually at one with this and amazingly safe in my space as part of that far grander whole. I feel it around me too ... the sense of communion, of community, the notion that we are all microscopic bits of something that has no beginning and no end ... at least not one that would disturb or have any impact on our forever places in the great plan. And the person next to me has the same short and yet—in a universe where time is a matter of perspective and in no way that we can understand—unquantifiable span. It is astounding, breathtaking to feel limitless, to feel part of a so much greater, impossible-to-measure whole. And for the first time, in a too-long time scarred with loss and grief and Pandemic and existential despair, under an ink-black sky into which is tucked an expanse that dwarfs the world as we know it, I feel warm; I feel safe; I feel expansive; I feel joy ... and I take that feeling home with me ... a sense of connection, even alone and in the midst of strangers in an oasis seemingly in the middle of nowhere under a garden of stars in the desert.

Author Biographies

Madeleine Adkins loves to write about her passions—food, cider, travel, identity, cultures and languages.

Originally from the San Francisco Bay Area, she's also lived in other parts of the US and abroad. Her nine-to-five career has included, among other things, intercultural communication training, user experience content design, and English teaching. The latter began with a two-and-a-half-year adventure in the Kansai region of Japan, where Madeleine dedicated her free time to studying the local language and shiatsu massage, and traveling the four main islands by train, bicycle and boat.

A linguist by training, she's spent a great deal of her life studying languages. She speaks a few of them—English, French, American Sign Language, Breton, and Japanese, and some rather rusty Irish—and can put together a few sentences in several others. As a linguist, she's conducted research in the *gaeltachts* (Irish speaking areas) of Ireland, including Donegal, Kerry and Mayo counties, and Belfast—studying the Irish language and the current efforts to keep the language alive. More recently, she's lived and traveled in Brittany, France, studying the Breton language and researching its community's efforts to revitalize it.

J. R. Barnett lives in Napa, California (though his heart is in Glen Ellen). As a child he would read the *World Book Encyclopedia*, volume-by-volume, A-Z, imagining experiencing all the places

Author Biographies

and meeting all the people he'd read about, and when done, start over and read it again. His thirst for new knowledge and experiences has not lessened with the years and miles, but his curiosity is now most often drawn backwards in time. He studies people, languages, art, histories, architecture, religions, beliefs and the like, gone for at least 1,000 years. Nothing pleases him more than sharing his wanderlust and reconstructive retrospective imaginings with a close-knit group of fellow-adventurers. Whether scaling cliff faces to explore ancient pueblo ruins, donning headlamps to crawl through Neolithic barrows, or sharing a pint in a snug once frequented by a literary great like Wolf, Tolkien, Austen, Dickens or a Brontë sister, Jim loves to share what he's learned about how things used to be, why, and most importantly why it should matter to us in the here and now.

Daphne Beyers grew up near Amish country in northeastern Pennsylvania, often finding herself caught in traffic behind wheel-and-buggy carriages. She's lived many places, including London, New York City, San Francisco, Berkeley and Palm Springs. Daphne taught herself to program at the age of thirteen and works as a computer consultant for various Fortune 500 companies. Her first essay, "Existential Cafe," was published in an award-winning anthology of Parisian stories, *Wandering in Paris: Luminaries and Love in the City of Light*.

Daphne's essays have also appeared in *Wandering in Cornwall: Mystery, Mirth and Transformation in the Land of Ancient Celts*, *Wandering in Andalusia: The Soul of Southern Spain*, and *Wandering in Greece: Athens, Islands and Antiquities*. Daphne currently lives in South Carolina with two Scottish terriers, Bhava and Haiku.

Hugh Biggar has been captivated by deserts since spending Christmas in the Sahara in Mali as a child, and by later reading *The Little Prince*. Since, he has continued to travel and chase ephemeral horizons. Memorable trips to desert hotspots include visiting the pyramids at Giza in Egypt, and canoeing through Big Bend in the Chihuahuan Desert. Along the way, he has worked as a reporter and for international agencies, and, at one point, the first Trader Joe's in the San Francisco Bay Area. His book on teaching in the Peace Corps in Poland is due out in 2025.

Michael J. Fitzgerald is a journalist and novelist whose home port is a floating house northwest of Portland, Oregon, on a tributary of the Willamette River.

His fifty-year journalism career includes stints at six daily newspapers in Northern and Central California and two wire services. Currently he writes a column titled "Write On" for a Geneva, New York, daily newspaper. While living in the San Francisco Bay Area, he wrote sailboat cruising tales for *Latitude 38* magazine and other sailing publications, including *Cruising World* and *Sail*.

He is writing a fourth ecothriller novel. Initially it will be released in serial form, via Substack.com. A traditional print version will be produced later.

Fitzgerald is a professor emeritus of journalism at California State University, Sacramento. He taught column writing, magazine writing and editing before retiring.

In the last decade, he drove from the West Coast to the East and back a half-dozen times, pulling a bright red teardrop trailer dubbed *The Red Writer*. His adventures and encounters have provided inspiration for his novels and fodder for his newspaper columns. (Michael.FitzgeraldFLTcolumnist@gmail.com)

Author Biographies

Peg Wendling Gerdes, a journal-writer since age seven, left the Midwest for San Francisco after college and found a treasure trove of things to ponder and write about throughout the West. She discovered early on that *writing it down* sharpens focus and forces deeper probing, both great strengths for a light-hearted, energetic person who flirts with many abiding interests.

Gerdes is known for published essays, long newsy communiques to friends, her constant drumbeat of letters to editors, politicians and community leaders on social justice, and for professional communications roles in companies and in her own consultancy. Favorite topics include the natural world, travel, gardening, gender, organizations, music, the grief of climate change, poetry, fantasy, hope, biographies, critters, birds and children's stories. Her books include *What's Working* (2012) and *Leaving Linear* (in progress). She is a leadership coach who helped companies flourish by harnessing the inherent restless power of their organizations, and now aims that competency at neighborhood and activist groups. She lives in cahoots with her husband Dave in Olympia, Washington.

Cyndi Goddard's travel adventures include six months sailing a 37-foot racer-cruiser from San Francisco Bay down the west coast of Mexico to Acapulco, a trip she chronicled in *Sail, Cruising World, Sailing, Latitude 38* and regional sailing publications.

In addition to sailing, Cyndi scuba dives, runs a small business consulting firm, practices yoga and kayaks. She has bungee jumped in Costa Rica; paddled Lago di Garda, Italy; explored wrecks and reefs in the Atlantic, Pacific and Caribbean; saluted the sun from a dock in Puerto Rico; and presented forecasts at board meetings.

In addition to the award-wining Wanderland Writers, Cyndi has worked with travel writer Don George, winning two awards for articles written in his workshops. She was twice selected to participate in the Community of Writers and The Writers Hotel conferences. She is a member of Left Coast Writers, Sisters in Crime and Mystery Writers of America. She is currently completing the first volume in her *Echoes* mystery series.

Thomas Harrell has joined the ranks of former lawyers turned writers. Since leaving the active practice of law, he has tried to turn lemons into lemonade and tried his hand at writing fiction instead of briefs (some might say they are not too dissimilar) and travel essays. His writing, both personal and travel related, often involves history, which he has always loved.

Tom most enjoys writing short stories and essays, but like so many writers dreams of completing a novel, most likely some improbable mash-up of history, fantasy, philosophy and humor, leavened with enough erotica to keep the pages turning.

His "Wandering" anthology stories reflect the special travel destinations steeped in history and culture; the diverse enthusiasms and encouragement of his fellow writers; and the "aha" moment that inspires every writer, and comes if you wander enough.

Born and raised in a small agricultural town on the central coast of California as half Mexican and half Japanese, **Naomi Lopez** grew up surrounded by strawberry fields and her Hispanic culture.

It wasn't until her trip to Japan as a volunteer English teacher and cultural ambassador that she got to explore her Asian roots for the first time. Her personal essay recounting the trip explores the

Author Biographies

concepts of cultural identity and belonging, and was recently published in *Confetti Travel Cafe.*

Naomi graduated from UCLA in spring 2023 with a B.A. in Philosophy and minors in Professional Writing and Environmental Systems & Society. Her professional writing capstone project explored various individuals' definitions of the meaning of life, based on their personal stories and life experiences. Throughout her undergraduate career, Naomi worked as both a copy editor and writer for multiple publications such as *The Daily Bruin, BruinLife* and *College Magazine.*

Naomi currently works as a writer at a talent immigration law firm in Los Angeles, and continues to write in her spare time about her passions—travel, culture and philosophy. Most recently, Naomi was selected as one of six participants for the 2024 Visit Greater Palm Springs "Meet the Mentors" Program.

Mary Jean (MJ) Pramik is the author of *Travels on the Edge: One Woman's Journeys on a Runaway Planet,* a collection of adventure travel stories with meditations on the climate crisis. MJ earned undergraduate and graduate degrees in biological sciences, completed an MFA in Writing, and has taught at San Francisco State University. Her science and travel articles and essays have appeared in *Nature Biotechnology, Cosmetic Surgery News, Good Housekeeping,* the *San Francisco Chronicle, Odyssey Magazine,* and the *National Enquirer.* She's contributed to Travelers' Tales' "Venturing in" and Wanderland Writers anthologies and has won several Solas Awards. A member of the Community of Writers and the American Academy of Poets, her poem "Rock, Stones" was nominated for a Pushcart Prize. MJ Pramik has hitchhiked across the US, fended off bill collectors in San Francisco, and counted bird carcasses along the Pacific's Point Reyes sands. Communicating with screeching penguins in Antarctica and swimming with South African sharks remain high points of her sojourn on this planet.

Anne Sigmon washed out of high school and college PE. After college, she headed for San Francisco and a communications career. Exotic travel was the stuff of dreams until, at 38, she married Jack, took tea with erstwhile headhunters in Borneo and climbed Mt. Kilimanjaro at 43. Five years later, she was zapped by a career-ending stroke caused by an obscure autoimmune disease called APS. She may be stuck with blood thinners and a damaged brain, but she still travels to the wild, from Botswana to Syria, Iran and Uzbekistan.

Anne's essays and award-winning travel stories have appeared in national publications including *Good Housekeeping* and *Stroke Connection* magazines and the American Heart Association website. Her work has appeared in digital magazines including Stories of Culture, Travel and the World; Best Travel Writing.com; and GeoEx.com; and more than a dozen anthologies, most recently Bradt Guide's *To Oldly Go* and *The Best Women's Travel Writing*.

Tatum Tomlinson is a high school student living in the Washington, D.C., area. She grew up in Indonesia, where she climbed volcanos, was chased by snakes, had dengue and typhoid fever, and snapped photos of crocodiles and Komodo dragons. She has been a competitive gymnast, art teacher for refugees, hiker and group leader. Drawing and creative writing remain favorite hobbies.

Author Biographies

Maw Shein Win's full-length poetry collection *Percussing the Thinking Jar* (Omnidawn) was published in Fall 2024. Her poetry collection *Storage Unit for the Spirit House* (Omnidawn, 2020) was nominated for the Northern California Book Award in Poetry, longlisted for the PEN America Open Book Award, and shortlisted for CALIBA's Golden Poppy Award for Poetry. She is the inaugural poet laureate of El Cerrito, California. Win's previous collections include *Invisible Gifts* and two chapbooks: *Ruins of a glittering palace* and *Score and Bone*. Win often collaborates with visual artists, musicians and other writers, and her Process Note Series features poets on their process. She teaches poetry in the MFA Program at the University of San Francisco. Along with Dawn Angelicca Barcelona and Mary Volmer, she is a co-founder of Maker, Mentor, Muse, a new literary community. mawsheinwin.com

You may find **Judy Zimola** messing around with art projects that have the potential for landing her in the ER; swimming in the San Francisco Bay; telling someone that they do, in fact, love to polka; and of course, writing. She's written for Traveler's Tales anthologies, *No Depression* magazine, *Green Living Arizona* magazine, and other publications. The only thing she likes better than seeing her stories in print is a long road trip on Nevada's forgotten highways. Unless it involves jail time, which was just that once and the result of a complete misunderstanding.

Editor Biographies

Linda Watanabe McFerrin is a poet, travel writer, novelist and contributor to numerous newspapers, magazines and anthologies. She is the author of two poetry collections, past editor of a popular Northern California guidebook and a winner of the Katherine Anne Porter Prize for Fiction. Her award-winning book-length fiction titles include *Namako: Sea Cucumber*, *The Hand of Buddha* and *Dead Love* (Stone Bridge Press, 2009), a Bram Stoker Award Finalist for Superior Achievement in a Novel. The most recent collection of her work, *Navigating the Divide* (Alan Squire Publishing, 2019), was a Next Generation Indie Book Awards Finalist. Her latest poetry collection, *POST-Apocalyptic Valentine* (7.13 Books) was published in September of 2024.

In addition, Linda has co-edited twelve anthologies, including the *Hot Flashes: sexy little stories & poems* series; judged the San Francisco Literary Awards, the Josephine Miles Award for Literary Excellence and the Kiriyama Prize; served as a visiting mentor for the Loft Mentor Series; and been guest faculty at the Oklahoma Arts Institute. A past NEA Panelist and juror for the Marin Literary Arts Council and the founder of Left Coast Writers®, she has led workshops in Greece, France, Italy, England, Ireland, Central America, Indonesia, Scotland, Spain and the United States, and has mentored a long list of accomplished writers and best-selling authors toward publication.

Joanna Biggar is a teacher, writer and traveler whose special places of the heart include the California coast and the South of France. As a professional writer for more than thirty years, she has written poetry, fiction, personal essays, features, news and travel articles for hundreds of publications including the *Washington Post Magazine, Psychology Today,* the *International Herald Tribune,* and the *Wall Street Journal.* A lifelong traveler, she has explored Indonesia, Costa Rica, Turkey, Québec Province in Canada, most recently Namibia, and of course, France. At home in Oakland, California, she continues to hike, garden, write and to enjoy the company of friends and fellow-travelers. She also continues to serve on the board of Oakland's Emiliano Zapata Street Academy, an alternative high school. *That Paris Year,* the first in a trilogy of novels, was published by Alan Squire Publishing in 2010, followed by *Melanie's Song* in 2019. The third novel, *To End All Wars,* will appear in 2025.

Editor Biographies

Laurie McAndish King writes about observing 20-foot-long Australian earthworms, tracking a three-eyed cannibal, and learning about an Ivy League astrophysicist's theory of how flying saucers are powered—not your typical travel writing. That's probably why *Kirkus Reviews* hails her as "an author with an eye for the quirky."

Her award-winning stories have appeared in the *Washington Post,* the *San Francisco Chronicle* and other magazines and literary anthologies. Her work has earned the Lowell Thomas Gold Award and a first-place award from *Smithsonian* magazine's photography contest.

Laurie's podcasts, some of which have aired on NPR, include talks with a futurist, ecologists, the co-founder of the Ethical Traveler, the first woman to row a boat single-handedly across three oceans, a Yale World Fellow, and a "frogmeister" at California's Calaveras County Jumping Frog Contest.

Laurie also wrote *An Erotic Alphabet* (for which she was dubbed "The Shel Silverstein of Erotica") and co-edited two books in the *Hot Flashes: sexy little stories & poems* series.

She is a past president of San Francisco Bay Area Travel Writers and a judge for the Northern California Chapter of the Society of Professional Journalists' Excellence in Journalism Awards. Laurie has an undergraduate degree in philosophy and a master's in education, and lives in northern California. (laurieking.com)

www.ingramcontent.com/pod-product-compliance
Lightning Source LLC
Chambersburg PA
CBHW060947050426
42337CB00052B/1632